Published by Simple Truths, an imprint of Sourcebooks
P.O. Box 4410, Naperville, Illinois 60567–4410
(630) 961-3900
sourcebooks.com

Cataloging-in-Publication Data is on file with the Library of Congress.

Printed and bound in China.
PP 10 9 8 7 6 5 4 3 2 1

To Dylan, Max, Wes, and Evan

"IMAGINATION IS MORE IMPORTANT THAN KNOWLEDGE."

—ALBERT EINSTEIN

WHY LISTEN TO
ALBERT EINSTEIN?

Albert Einstein was born in Germany in 1879. In 1905, while working as a patent clerk in Bern, Switzerland, Einstein published four academic papers that revolutionized the entirety of physics. These papers included his famous equation, $E=mc^2$, which ushered in the atomic age. He was awarded the Nobel Prize in Physics in 1921 for his pioneering contributions to quantum physics before his more famous predictions from his theory of relativity were verified. Suffice it to say, when Einstein spoke, people listened.

WHY DID HE SAY THIS?

Einstein is rightly considered the greatest scientific mind ever to have existed. His uniquely insightful contributions to human knowledge cannot be done justice with words alone. Yet, for Einstein, knowledge was not paramount—it was just a by-product of a healthy imagination.

But let's not just accept these words because Einstein was a genius. Good science requires a critical analysis of our own biases and those we have borrowed from others. We should be clear first on what knowledge is, or at least what it meant to Einstein. Knowledge is sometimes understood to mean facts. In this view, someone who has memorized an encyclopedia, which contains a lot of information, has a lot of knowledge. This is not the only definition of knowledge, though.

Knowledge can mean understanding. A computer can store the contents of an encyclopedia, but we would not say the computer *understands* that information. Understanding occurs when we can answer the *why* question about the facts. When we know why the facts must be the way they are, then we have understanding.

What Einstein was saying, in these terms, is that *understanding* is more important than *knowing*. Einstein developed his great understanding of the world by thinking through hypothetical situations that he called "thought experiments." In other words, he used his imagination to obtain understanding.

BE AN EINSTEIN

Knowledge, in the sense of facts, is easy to come by today. With the internet, we have access to an unimaginable amount of information at our fingertips. However, this does not mean that there are more people with understanding today than in Einstein's time. In fact, it might be quite the opposite.

The ease with which we can obtain knowledge has led to a situation where many people never think for themselves about why things must be as they are. They just accept what they read on the internet or hear from other people without question. As a result, these people do not develop their own understanding and remain ignorant of many important issues in life.

In order to become truly knowledgeable, you must learn how to use your imagination like Einstein did—to develop original thoughts and ideas based on your current understanding of the world around you.

You can follow Einstein and hone your imaginative skills with these three tips.

1. PRACTICE "WHAT IF?"

Einstein's thought experiments were all based on the question, "What if?" He would imagine what would happen in a world that was different from ours in some key way. By doing so, he was able to see the world in a new light and develop new understandings.

You can do the same thing. The next time you encounter a problem, ask yourself, "What if?" and change some key assumptions, no matter how far-fetched it might sound. For example, "What if I could fly?" or "What if I had a million dollars?" By changing your perspective in this way, you may be able to see the problem in a new light and find a creative solution.

Say you are a manager of a fast-food restaurant, and you need to increase customer response time at the drive-through. You might ask yourself, "What if my employees could work from home?" even if this isn't actually a workable option. So why ask it, then? Well, what if they really were at home? How could you make it work? They would surely need to see the cars from their homes as they approach the restaurant. Wait a minute! You could put a camera in your drive-through lane. In fact, you could install two-way cameras so the customers could see and hear the employees. Genius—and all because of a hypothetical question.

2. TAKE A BREAK FROM THE PROBLEM.

Have you ever been working on a problem late at night and found yourself making little to no progress? Have you ever, instead of burning the midnight oil, gone to bed and gotten a good night's rest only to find, in the morning, you have a new insight?

When you're stuck on a problem, it can be helpful to take a break from it. Go for a walk, take a shower, take a nap, or just step away from the problem for a while. This will give your mind a chance to relax and allow your imagination to take over.

Einstein himself was famous for taking daily walks—and no, he didn't bring his mobile phone with him! Einstein would walk by himself or with colleagues and visitors of his Princeton office. Some of his deepest insights were obtained or given to him on these walks.

Imagine you are a software developer, and you've been struggling to find a bug in your code. Instead of working through your frustration, you could take a walk around the block to clear your head. As you are walking, you notice an orange door you hadn't before. Your mind starts to wander. You think about how orange paint is made and remember orange is a secondary color, and so must be made of primary colors. Then it dawns on you that the bug is *not* in the secondary code you've been looking at. You head back to your computer and fix the bug in the primary code. If you had stayed at your desk, frustrated, it's unlikely you would have come up with this solution.

3. BE OPEN TO NEW IDEAS.

If you want to develop new understandings, you need to be open to new ideas. This means being willing to question your existing beliefs and assumptions. It also means being open to unique and different ways of looking at the world.

Of course, it is important not to blindly accept every new idea that comes along. But if you never question your beliefs, you will never learn anything new or develop any deeper understanding of the world around you.

Let's say you are a parent, and your child is reluctant to go to school. You might have a host of assumptions and even accusations for this behavior, but what else might be going on? Start by observing your child and trying to see the world from their perspective. Try to find out what your child sees that you don't. What are their fears and concerns? What do they enjoy about school? The perspective of a child might seem far removed from models of reality adults live by, but it is their world, and understanding it can only be truly achieved by accepting a new (or perhaps old) perspective.

THE SCIENCE

In an article titled "The Role of Thought Experiments in Science and Science Learning," Stephens and Clement (2012) concluded that, in a study of middle and high school students, the spontaneous use of imaginative thought experiments was a skill used by advanced students and concluded that "imagistic simulation may be a very important sense-making process."

Supported by numerous studies, psychologists seem to agree that stepping away from a problem is beneficial in coming up with creative solutions. Like most things to do with the seemingly infinite complexity of the human mind, we don't yet have a consensus on *why* it works—though, of course, many theories exist, as discussed by Gilhooly in a 2016 *Frontiers in Psychology* article. Much of the work is thus focused on devising techniques to improve and accurately measure the effect.

In a 2018 report, Epstein, Schmidt, and Warfel demonstrated that games and exercises developed to strengthen proficiency in creative skills, such as capturing and recording new ideas, increased the rate of new idea generation by 55 percent after as long as eight months in a group of seventy-four people. The organization the people worked for claimed the activity had netted it over $4 million. So it seems imagination is more important than money as well!

By following the preceding tips, you can develop your imagination and become more like Einstein. Who knows—you may even come up with some groundbreaking new insights of your own.

"NOTHING IN LIFE IS TO BE FEARED, IT IS ONLY TO BE UNDERSTOOD."

NOW IS THE TIME TO UNDERSTAND MORE,

SO THAT WE MAY FEAR LESS."

—MARIE CURIE

WHY LISTEN TO
MARIE CURIE?

Marie Curie, born in Poland in 1867, was a physicist and chemist who conducted pioneering research on radioactivity. She was the first woman to win a Nobel Prize and the only person to win the prize in two different scientific fields, chemistry and physics. Curie was an intellectual giant who overcame many obstacles to pioneer a path in science. Much of our understanding of the atomic world, including its use in medicine, is either due directly to Curie or is derived from her work. It's unlikely that Curie was literally fearless, but she came close.

WHY DID SHE SAY THIS?

We can all identify with a fear of the unknown. Anxiety is a normal emotion that everyone experiences at some point in their life. It can be triggered by various things, such as an upcoming test, a job interview, or a first date. While a certain amount of anxiety is normal and even helpful, too much anxiety can be debilitating.

But Curie did not believe that fear and uncertainty are a necessary pair. In other words, Curie's philosophy was that fear should not limit our desire to understand the unknown. When faced with the unknown, she didn't let her fear stop her from investigating. Instead, she used her curiosity to drive her research. As a result, she made many important discoveries that have helped improve the lives of people worldwide.

Unfortunately, the context around this quote included the fact that she had recently discovered she had cancer. At the time, it was not known that working so closely with radioactive substances was the likely cause. (Note that her notebooks are still radioactive today and shielded in lead boxes!) But Curie did not fear her diagnosis because she knew that knowledge and understanding could eliminate the uncertainty.

This quote speaks to the power of true knowledge. When we understand something, we are less likely to be afraid of it. Curie's words encourage us to push past our fears and learn as much as we can about the world around us.

BE A CURIE

Curie's words are as relevant today as they were when she spoke them over a century ago. In today's world, we are faced with many unknowns. Sometimes it can feel like there is too much to fear and not enough to understand. But if we take a cue from Marie Curie, we can use our curiosity to help us overcome our fears and expand our understanding of the world around us.

Fear can be a powerful emotion that prevents us from reaching our full potential. But if we channel our fear into curiosity, we can turn it into a force for good. So the next time you feel anxious or afraid, remember Marie Curie's words and use your curiosity to help you understand the unknown.

You can follow Curie and let go of your fear with these three tips.

1. EDUCATE YOURSELF.

One of the best ways to overcome fear is to educate yourself. When you understand something, it is no longer as scary. So, if you're afraid of something, take the time to learn about it. Read books, watch videos, or talk to someone who knows more about the subject than you.

Curie, of course, didn't watch videos or listen to podcasts, but she was an ardent reader and educated herself in her spare time. She could not initially afford the tuition at the University of Paris, but studied anyway by reading books, exchanging letters, and receiving tutoring while organizing the necessary funds.

To help picture the application of Curie's advice, let's say you're afraid of public speaking and have been asked to give a speech at your best friend's wedding. Clearly you can't decline, but you can hardly bear the thought of freezing on stage. Here is where education comes in. You can learn about public speaking and understand what makes you anxious. Maybe it is that you think people will laugh at you. Now that you know what your fear is, you can tackle it head on. You find a great tip—choose two friends in the audience that you can rely on making eye contact with. If you get nervous, you can always go back to looking at these friends. This idea soothes your fears, and you deliver the perfect speech, creating a wonderful memory for your best friend.

2. FACE YOUR FEARS.

Another way to overcome fear is to face it head-on. If you're afraid of heights, for example, don't avoid tall buildings—go to the top of one. If you're afraid of public speaking and aren't forced to do it, don't avoid speaking in front of people—volunteer to give a presentation. By facing your fears, you will slowly start to overcome them.

Curie faced her fears and overcame them. She was a

woman in science in the nineteenth century, a time when science was considered a man's domain. Undeterred by these odds and her own inexperience in research, Curie carried out groundbreaking experiments that led to important discoveries about radioactivity.

Suppose you are a freelance web designer and due to attend the biggest conference of the year, but you are afraid of attending the networking events. You know you should attend, but your palms start sweating at the very thought. At this point, you can either resolve to not go, telling yourself that it is better than humiliation, or you can face your fear head-on. You choose the latter, but you don't dive straight into the networking event. You face your fear in baby steps by attending as many small networking events as possible before the big show. While your fear isn't completely eliminated, at least your palms aren't sweating. You shake the hand of a big client who knows your portfolio, and meeting you in person sealed the deal.

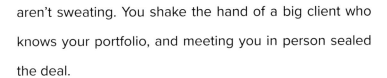

3. TALK ABOUT YOUR FEARS.

Marie Curie's biography, written by her daughter Eve Curie, contains excerpts of many letters written to her siblings and daughters expressing her fears. "Sometimes my courage fails me," she wrote to her sister, but ultimately, "I could not live without the laboratory."

Sometimes, the best way to overcome fear is to talk about it. When you share your fears with someone else, they can provide support and understanding. This can help you to feel less alone and more capable of dealing with your fears. It's not likely that the other person has a secret phrase or can prescribe medicine to eliminate your fear, but sometimes simply expressing it in words can remove some uncertainty.

Imagine you have started a recent relationship with a zookeeper. This sounds pretty cool to you, except for a small problem: they take care of the creepy-crawly things at the zoo, and you happen to have a fear of spiders. Coupled with that, you are also afraid to tell your new partner that you fear the one thing they love! You decide to confide in your best friend, who suggests you go on a double date where they will provide moral support. During the date, you reveal your fear. The others agree. And your partner? Well, they confess a fear of spiders as well! You resolve to overcome your fear together.

THE SCIENCE

We all have—or think we have—an intuitive idea of what *fear* is, but the biology of it is rather complex. Is fear a conscious state? Is it an emotion? Is it a behavior? These are the questions biologists worry about, and we won't have the answers anytime soon. In the meantime, clinicians rely on self-reporting for obvious reasons— would any answer to the above questions make you feel better about a spider crawling on you if you were arachnophobic? (That's the technical term for fear of spiders, by the way.) More relevant to our example, the technical term for a fear of laughter is geloto-phobia, and it is an affecting fear across many cultures.

In a recent review article in the *Journal of Anxiety Disorders*, Carleton argues that *fear of the unknown* is the one and only fundamental fear from which all others derive. This implies that treatments aimed at reducing this fear can help to eliminate other fears. Mahoney and McEvoy suggest that "enhancing tolerance of uncertainty may play a role in the optimal management of social phobia." Optimal! Now that is a strong conclusion for a scientific paper. Apparently, Curie was a century ahead of her time!

Exposure therapy is a clinical technique that exposes patients to their source of fear in an environment with minimal to no danger. An example is becoming comfortable with heights using virtual reality. Exposure therapy is one of the most popular and successful therapies for a variety of anxiety disorders. A group of psychologists from the University of Bergen, Norway, performed a meta-analysis of studies reporting on psychological interventions for fear of public speaking. The studies totaled over 1,300 participants, and it was found that even technology-driven exposure therapies delivered online and in virtual environments were effective.

Talking about fears is an often-recommended method to

alleviate anxiety. However, psychologists at the University of California, Los Angeles, found that specifically labeling your experiences and emotions was more effective than attempting to downplay them. Participants who were afraid of spiders used several techniques while the researchers measured how close they were able to get to a live tarantula. Those who said things like "I'm anxious and terrified" were able to get much closer (and had a smaller emotional response as measured by skin conductance) than those who said things like "It's just a small spider that can't hurt me" or nothing at all. It seems honesty in vocalizing your fears is the key to success.

If you're afraid of something, don't let it control your life. Follow Curie's advice and take steps to overcome your fears through understanding.

"LIFE NEED NOT BE EASY, PROVIDED ONLY THAT IT IS NOT EMPTY."

—LISE MEITNER

WHY LISTEN TO
LISE MEITNER?

Born in Vienna, Austria, in 1878, Meitner was one of the first women to earn a PhD in physics from the University of Vienna. After graduation, she moved to Berlin, where she worked with some of the most renowned physicists of her time, including Otto Hahn, who became a longtime friend and collaborator. Together they discovered nuclear fission, the principle behind nuclear reactors and weapons. For this reason, Meitner is often referred to as "the mother of nuclear fission."

WHY DID SHE SAY THIS?

A Jewish woman living in Austria during the rise of the Nazi Party, Meitner was forced to flee her country and leave behind her life's work. But she didn't give up. In the face of adversity, Meitner persevered and continued her research. She went on to make important contributions to the understanding of nuclear fission, a discovery that would change the world forever.

The work on fission was recognized for a Nobel Prize in 1944, but Meitner did not receive it. The prize was solely given to Hahn. However, she was not bitter about this. She continued her work and was eventually recognized among her peers for her contributions to science later in life.

Lise Meitner was the unsung hero of the discovery of nuclear fission. Although she was not widely recognized for her contributions to science until after her death, Meitner's legacy is now widely known. She was a brilliant scientist who significantly contributed to our understanding of the atomic world.

Through all the hardships she encountered in her life, Meitner showed that it is possible to overcome adversity and continue to lead a meaningful life. Despite the difficulties she faced, she did not give up or let empty distractions consume her. Instead, Meitner persisted and focused on what was most important to her: making valuable contributions to science.

BE A MEITNER

The quote from Meitner is a reminder that life is not always easy. There will be times when we face challenges and difficulties. But it is important to remember that these challenges can make life richer and more meaningful. It is through overcoming hardship that we grow and develop as people.

In today's social media–driven world, it is easy to fall into the trap of comparing ourselves to others. We see posts about other people's successes and think, "Why don't I have that?" or "What am I doing wrong?" This kind of thinking only leads to feelings of insecurity and inadequacy. Instead of comparing yourself to others, focus on your own progress and journey. Celebrate your own successes. Remember that everyone has their unique path in life, so you don't need to compare yourself to anyone else.

With these three tips, you can channel Meitner's optimism into your own success.

1. FOCUS ON WHAT YOU CAN CONTROL.

When you're facing a difficult situation, it can be easy to get caught up in everything that is out of your control. But this will only make you feel more powerless and stressed. Instead, focus on the things that you can control. What are the steps that you can take to improve the situation? What are the things that you can do to make yourself feel better? What can you do to endure?

By any usual measure, Meitner had every right to begrudge the treatment she faced throughout her life. We remember those scientists who were the loudest or most eccentric, forgetting that most were simply ordinary or crashed and burned in their attempts to have their names immortalized. But not Meitner—she was truly different. She remained focused on what gave meaning to her life— physics. By doing so, she didn't need to rely on prizes or fame, as her status within the scientific community only ever grew.

Suppose you are about to enter a sales meeting with your boss, and you are feeling nervous because you have to give the pitch. You start thinking about all of the things that could go wrong—what if they don't like me? What will my boss think of me? This negative thinking only increases your anxiety levels. But then you remember that you can't control these things. The only thing you can control is your performance. With this in mind, you walk into the meeting with confidence and nail the pitch. You may or may not have landed the new client, but you got a thumbs-up from your boss.

2. BUILD YOUR NETWORK.

Meitner was able to continue her work despite being

exiled from her home country. This was possible only because she had a strong network of friends and colleagues who supported her and tirelessly fought to secure her a new home outside of Germany.

When you're facing a difficult situation, reach out to your network of family and friends. These are the people who will support you and help you get through tough times. Still network-building? Keep at it. Meaningful relationships take time to develop but are critical to your success.

Let's say you are a recent college graduate who is struggling to find a job. You've been sending out resumes and attending networking events, but you're not getting any bites. It can be tempting to give up or feel like you're the only one in this situation. But instead of wallowing in self-pity, you reach out to your network of family and friends. An old friend from high school, with whom you made a continued effort to keep in touch, happens to be working with your dream company. They put in a good word for you, and the next thing you know, you've landed an interview.

3. MAINTAIN HUMILITY.

Meitner was a brilliant scientist, but she was always humble about her achievements. When going through a difficult time, it can be tempting to become bitter and resentful, especially if you are confident in your abilities. But this will only make the situation worse. Instead, try to maintain your humility. Focus on the things you are grateful for, which will help you see the good in the world and your life.

Though her research led directly to the creation of the atomic bomb, Meitner publicly denounced it and refused to help develop the program. The inscription on her tomb-stone reads, "Lise Meitner: a physicist who never lost her humanity." She saw the best in herself and in other people, even when others did not.

Imagine you are an up-and-coming artist. Your work is part of an exhibition—your first reception, in fact. You are proud and, perhaps, feeling a little boastful. You notice another eager artist enthusiastically promoting his piece to a potential buyer. He nearly knocks the drink out of their hand with his bravado. Eventually his aggression pays off, and he convinces a timid couple to buy the work. You calm your nerves as the original buyer now approaches your piece. You stand in silence and allow them to fully appreciate it. Then they turn to you and say, "amazing," and ask what you think of it. Instead of providing a glowing review of your own work, you talk instead about the challenging and emotional inspiration behind it. The buyer is moved but reveals they are not actually a buyer—they are an international art critic!

THE SCIENCE

"Optimistic" is sometimes a generic label for people who display a carefree attitude to life, which is usually caricatured beyond believability in fiction. But people can be carefree without being optimistic. Technically speaking, optimism comes in degrees and measures the extent to which a person has favorable expectations of future events. It is scientifically linked with subjective well-being in times of difficulty. There is a common misconception that people are born as either optimists or pessimists, but studies refute this.

For example, Seligman, Schulman, and Tryon demonstrated the opposite in a controlled trial, that pessimistic attitudes can change with appropriate intervention.

The notion of social networks might seem new in the social media age, but it only takes a moment of thought to realize that they have existed since...well, as long as people. It's only in the past several decades, though, that researchers have studied them. As expected, having a network is a good thing. In fact, researchers don't spend time on the obvious, so most studies on the topic of social networks focus on nuances like how to measure network size, structure, ranking, and the correlation of each with specific quantities. The result of numerous studies seems to show that different qualities of a social network have distinct effects. For example, Zou and Ingram studied the professional networks of managers and found that creativity and decision-making were improved when networks had only weak connections across the organizational boundary, but strong connections *within* the organization were required for superior task execution performance.

While most research is not so conclusive as to make specific recommendations for how a particular person's network should look, the generic advice is simple: you should at least have a core part of your network with strong connections built on trust. OK, great, so how do you do it? *Networking* is the active attempt to both build and maintain a social network. De Janasz and Forret developed some techniques that enhanced the networking capabilities of students, which are now mirrored in advice outside of academic journals—namely, practice in simulated situations and environments.

Ultimately, building those strong relationships requires trust and cooperation, which can be seen as a natural by-product of humility. Psychologists from Virginia Commonwealth University call this the *social bonds hypothesis*. They have observed evidence that humility promotes cooperative alliances in both personal and professional relationships as well as leads to better overall health outcomes.

So next time you face a difficult situation, put your ego away and remember Meitner's words. A full and rewarding life comes from facing and overcoming adversity.

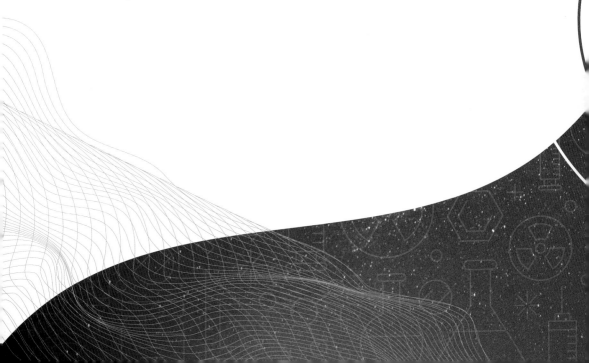

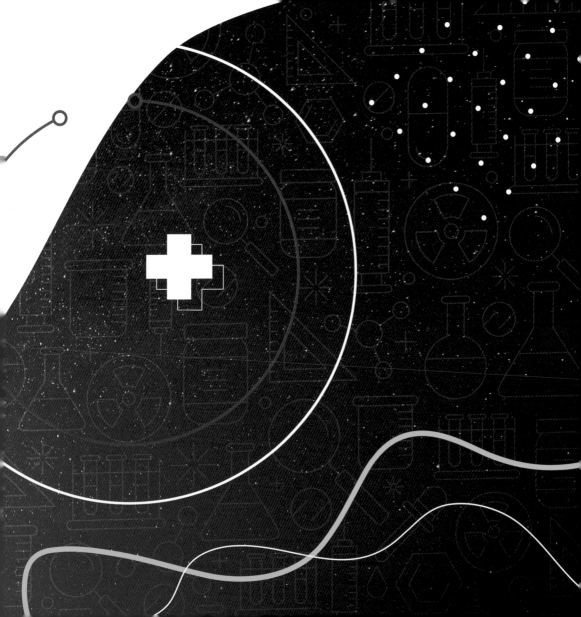

YOU CAN ONLY HELP HIM FIND IT WITHIN HIMSELF."

—GALILEO GALILEI

WHY LISTEN TO
GALILEO?

Galileo Galilei (known better as simply Galileo) was an Italian physicist born in 1564. He made significant contributions to physics and engineering, developing the law of inertia and the principle of relative motion, both of which are fundamental to physics. He was the first to use a telescope to study the night sky, and he made many important discoveries about the planets and stars. Indeed, he is best known for his work on astronomy, discovering the phases of Venus, the largest moons of Jupiter, and the rings of Saturn. You'd definitely want to listen to Galileo unless you were the sixteenth-century church, in which case you would imprison him for being a heretic. Not cool!

WHY DID HE SAY THIS?

Galileo was a great scientist and philosopher who made important contributions to our understanding of the universe, but he was also a master teacher. In this quote, he stresses the importance of helping students discover knowledge for themselves rather than simply trying to teach them facts. But you can also apply this wisdom to your own life and learning journey.

Of course, we can force the memorization of facts upon ourselves, but the results would be temporary at best. It is better to spend time developing the tools necessary to discover, understand, and assimilate new knowledge. This is true in all areas of life, not just in science.

Galileo carefully observed the night sky to see the truths of the universe for himself during a time when such facts were extremely unfashionable. In his time, it was believed that the Earth was the center of everything. By observing the phases of Venus, Galileo witnessed that it rotated around the sun. By discovering the moons of Jupiter, Galileo witnessed that other planets were the centers of orbiting objects.

The facts were clear to Galileo: the Earth was not the center of the universe. But there was no way to teach these facts to people within the predominant system at the time. However, Galileo could show anyone willing to look through his telescopes what truly was.

BE A GALILEO

This quote is even more relevant today than it was in Galileo's time. In the internet age, we have access to more information than ever. Just as students today don't need to be spoon-fed facts, we too can look them up ourselves, provided we can critically evaluate the sources available to us.

Students need help from their teachers to make sense of all this information. They need help in identifying the best tools for discovering knowledge for themselves. This applies to our own self-teaching as well. Before seeking facts, we must be sure that we are equipped to evaluate their accuracy or at least apply a healthy dose of skepticism.

If you want to learn as if taught by Galileo, here are three tips.

1. ASK LOTS OF QUESTIONS.

Be curious about the world around you and ask questions. Delve deeper into the things that interest you and never be satisfied with superficial answers. Ask how things work and why they are the way they are. By being curious, you will develop a love for learning and the skills of knowledge discovery.

Galileo was more than an astronomer. He was also a mathematician, physicist, and engineer. He was curious about everything, and his curiosity led him to make important discoveries. If Galileo had been content with the answers he received from authorities, he may have never made his discoveries. He was constantly asking questions and looking for evidence to support or disprove what he believed or was told.

Imagine you are an investigative journalist who has finally received your own beat. You've been assigned to write a story on a new type of battery that is being developed by a local company. A naive writer would let the company bully them into printing their sales pitch, but not you. You say you are not satisfied without evidence and demand you be able to take it home overnight to test the claims of the battery's longevity. The company reluctantly agrees, and you now have twenty-four hours to verify the data they've given you. You are a curious person, so you do more than just test the battery. You also contact experts on the technology, look up the company's published research, and interview people who have worked on the science. In the end, you have a fair and balanced article that wins praise from your readers and peers.

2. BE PATIENT.

Galileo believed that learning was a slow and gradual process. He was patient with his students and allowed them the time they needed to understand new concepts. Galileo was also patient with himself. He invented better and better telescopes as he made and remade observations of celestial objects over several years before coming to his conclusions.

You should be patient with yourself, too. Learning takes time, so be patient and don't get discouraged. When you discover a new fact or tool, go back and reexamine previous assumptions to refine your understanding.

Consider the following scenario. You are a software developer who has been asked to create a new time management app for your company. The project is complex, and you have never built anything like it before. You could build something quick that works, but instead, you interview your colleagues in the company to understand the needs of the app's users. It is exhausting, but your patience pays off. Not only did you build a functional product, your colleagues appreciate the effort you put into listening to their needs.

3. DON'T GIVE UP.

Galileo was a persistent man. He didn't give up when faced with challenges. He continued to experiment and observe, even when others doubted him. A famous story goes that Galileo climbed the Tower of Pisa and dropped two stone balls of different sizes, which—to the amazement of onlookers—landed at the same time.

You should also be persistent in your pursuit of knowledge and resist giving up when things get tough. Be willing to change your mind when presented with evidence that contradicts your beliefs, but don't give up easily on what you believe is true. Remember that learning is an ongoing process, so keep investigating even after you think you have all the answers.

Suppose you are an author who has been asked to review a new book. The author is an expert on the subject, but you quickly realize that the book is full of errors. You could write a scathing review, but instead, you decide to reach out to the author and offer your help in correcting the mistakes. Your persistence pays off when the print edition is published and receives positive reviews from critics. Meanwhile, you've earned a strong reputation with the publisher and new ally.

THE SCIENCE

They say curiosity killed the cat, but it definitely didn't hurt its memory. Neuroscientists from the University of California at Davis showed that motivated curiosity excited brain regions associated with pleasure and the parts of the brain thought to be responsible for the creation of memories. Study participants who ranked as "curious knowledge-seekers" were also better able to remember information presented to them that was unrelated to the series of trivia questions they were asked. If you are curious about this research, you've already taken the first step!

The same people that judge cats' curiosity might also have said "patience is a virtue." Affirmations to put on motivational posters aside, Schnitker and Emmons have demonstrated that patient people experience fewer negative emotions and feel more gratitude...which is great, but sunshine and roses aren't going to pay the bills. In a landmark study published in *Nature*, Liu and colleagues studied the works of many artists, film directors, and scientists to find that success occurred in spurts ("hot streaks") and happened randomly throughout their careers. In essence, had these individuals given up at any point, they would not have seen success. They displayed the patience required to practice their craft and eventually be productive enough to find favorable outcomes. However, of the 30,000 individual careers analyzed, a whopping 90 percent had at least one hot streak. In other words, you might not know when success will come, but if you are patient, it eventually will.

Patience often requires endurance, especially in trying times. This is related closely to what psychologist Carol S. Dweck calls a *growth mindset,* or "passion for stretching yourself and sticking to it, even (or especially) when it's not going well." This is to be contrasted with a *fixed mindset,* which is a belief that skills and intelligence are innate and inflexible. In a 2019 *Nature* article, Dweck and her colleagues reported on a national study of high school students who were presented with a short intervention promoting a growth mindset, which improved grades and enrollment in more advanced classes. In effect, the intervention showed students how to see success within themselves, just as Galileo predicted centuries ago.

Whether you are training others or just yourself, be a teacher like Galileo—be curious, patient, and persistent in your learning. By doing so, you will discover the true joy of discovery.

"LUCK IS A COMBINATION OF PREPARATION AND OPPORTUNITY.

IF YOU'RE PREPARED AND THE OPPORTUNITY COMES UP, IT'S YOUR GOOD FORTUNE TO HAVE BEEN

IN THE RIGHT PLACE AT THE RIGHT TIME AND TO HAVE BEEN PREPARED FOR THE JOB."

—KATHERINE JOHNSON

WHY LISTEN TO
KATHERINE JOHNSON?

Katherine Johnson was a mathematician who worked for NASA during the early years of the space program. She was responsible for calculating the trajectories of space missions, and her work was critical to the success of many historic spaceflights. As the most trusted "human computer," she verified the trajectory of the Apollo 11 mission, which was the first moon landing.

WHY DID SHE SAY THIS?

Johnson was born in 1918 in West Virginia, at a time and place when non-white children were unable to attend school beyond the seventh grade. This was also a time in America when women were not expected to pursue a career at all, let alone in mathematics. Being both Black and female, this was only the beginning of a lifetime of societal barriers that she faced. At a very high level, then, it would seem that Johnson's life and career were full of lucky breaks—but the details reveal that her luck was well-calculated.

Johnson attributed her success to the result of being prepared for opportunities when they presented themselves. For example, Johnson was offered a full scholarship to West Virginia State College, enrolling as one of the first non-white persons in mathematics. Was it luck? Not entirely. Johnson recognized her own talent and passion for math at a young age. Even when facing barriers that barred her from formal study, she made sure to stay sharp by doing mental calculations. Of course, she did not expect a full scholarship, but she made sure she was prepared when the opportunity arose.

It might also seem lucky that a person with no experience in the aerospace industry would come to be one of the most important people at NASA. NASA grew out of a small team of research engineers at the Langley Research Center, where Johnson worked as a "human computer." The team needed some temporary help with calculations, and Johnson accepted the invitation. She made herself indispensable, and she quietly became a permanent member of an otherwise all-male task force. Then, when NASA announced they would land a human on the moon that decade, Johnson was already there to do the calculations necessary to make it happen.

Johnson was a true trailblazer with a career full of firsts. How does one get so lucky so often? Johnson knew, and she gave away the secret: preparation.

BE A JOHNSON

Johnson's advice is simple but profound. While it requires an element of luck, opportunities can only be seized by those who have put in the hard work—those who are prepared. You can't control when the opportunity will come, but you can control how prepared you are and put yourself on the best path to receive them.

Johnson's advice is especially relevant in today's world, where the pace of change is accelerating and the competition for opportunities is fierce. You need to put in the hard work up front so that you're ready when opportunities come your way. Success always looks like luck, but on closer inspection, we can see that luck is engineered.

To seem as if you have the foresight of Johnson, follow these three tips.

1. TAKE THE UNBEATEN PATH.

Johnson wanted to work for the space program but missed the application deadline. Instead of waiting for another year, she applied to the airplane program and worked her way up until an internal opportunity presented itself from within the organization.

If you, too, want to be prepared for opportunities, you need to stay open-minded. This means being willing to try new things and think outside the box. It also means being open to change and new ideas. By staying open-minded, you'll be more likely to see and seize opportunities when they come your way.

Say you are an independent designer and a new company moves in next door to your studio. They are in need of a website, and they come to you for help. The trouble is that you don't have the web development skills to build a website from scratch. So, you can either turn them down because you don't do that kind of work, or you can take the opportunity to learn something new and build the website for them. Staying open-minded, you agree to build their website. In the end, the website looks great, you've learned a new skill, and you gained a new client for your primary business.

2. BE RESILIENT.

When Johnson wanted to join the space program briefings, she was told that women didn't typically attend. However, since there was no actual rule against it, she persisted and opened up new opportunities that existed only behind those otherwise closed doors.

Like Johnson, you can't just sit around and wait for opportunities to come to you. You need to be proactive and go out and find them. This means being willing to take risks and put yourself out there. It also means being persistent and not giving up when things get tough.

Imagine you are working as a marketing assistant at a small company. The company has been around for a long time and has a loyal customer base. However, there is no real social media presence. You have some great ideas for how to market the company's products and services to a wider audience, but your boss won't commit any resources to them. You could give up and accept that things are never going to change. Or you could take matters into your own hands and start implementing your ideas on your own time, which is, of course, what you do! Your social media strategy takes off, and your boss starts to take notice of your efforts and asks that you implement them in other parts of the business.

3. PRACTICE.

When it comes down to it, preparation is practice. Practicing skills, training, and seeking improvement are key, but when it comes to opportunities you don't want to miss, you can prepare in a more directed way. Simulate the opportunity in advance so you're familiar with the situation and know what to do when the time comes.

Johnson and the other "human computers" were some of the most well-practiced mathematicians in the history of the world. Johnson herself said her love of the work led to fourteen-hour days of calculations. Before John Glenn's historic mission to become the first American to orbit the Earth, NASA used new IBM computers to calculate the trajectory. But Glenn would only board that flight if Johnson personally verified the calculations. It took her an entire day, but the numbers came out the same, and Glenn became an instant hero.

Now, you don't have to practice mathematics with cold-war urgency, but the fact remains—the more you practice, the better prepared you will be. For example, let's say you are a freshly graduated software engineer and are hoping to land a job in a certain big tech company. Instead of going in blind, you research the company's hiring practices. You find out that the interview will involve a software coding exercise in a programming language you aren't familiar with. So, you practice for that specific interview by learning the new language and working through practice problems. When the interview finally comes, you nail it.

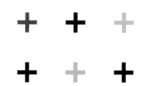

THE SCIENCE

In his book *The Luck Factor*, psychologist Richard Wiseman describes a ten-year study of self-proclaimed lucky people. He found that good fortune was largely ruled by four things: skill at creating and noticing opportunities, following intuition, having positive expectations, and staying resilient. The former two are skills that require intentional development whereas the latter two relate to mindset, though all require practice.

The notion of preparation depends very much on the opportunities you hope to capitalize on. For example, if you're hoping to become a professional athlete, you'll need years of training and practice. But if you're hoping to start your own business, you may only need to put in a few months of research and planning. A meta-analysis of eighty-eight scientific studies on practice and skill found a considerable difference in its effectiveness depending on the skill in question. For athletes, practice explained 18 percent of the variation in performance, while for professions, it only accounted for 1 percent.

The infamous "10,000 hour rule," which states that this number of hours of deliberate practice is sufficient to become an expert at anything, came from a research article by psychologist Anders Ericsson that studied specifically elite violinists. The average number of hours of practice the participants in the study had was 10,000. However, if your goal is something less high-stakes, such as memorizing numbers, you can reach world-class performance levels after only a few hundred hours of practice.

The idea of practicing the memorization of digits might not sound compelling, but this is where resilience comes in. In a separate study of National Spelling Bee competitors, it was found that the "most effortful and least enjoyable" method of preparation was the one most favored by the best competitors because of its effectiveness. The technique in question was the most obvious one: memorizing words. Other techniques, including reading for pleasure and practicing in social groups, were more enjoyable but ultimately less effective. That all being said, every participant at the National Spelling Bee is a stellar speller because of some level of practice—but it's grittier ones who win.

Though there are never any guarantees, following Johnson can maximize your chances of seizing opportunities when they come your way.

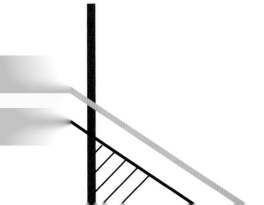

"SHALL I REFUSE MY DINNER BECAUSE I DO NOT FULLY UNDERSTAND...

THE PROCESS OF DIGESTION?"

—OLIVER HEAVISIDE

WHY LISTEN TO
OLIVER HEAVISIDE?

Oliver Heaviside lived at the turn of the nineteenth century and was an English mathematician and physicist. He made great theoretical advances in the study of electricity and magnetism. By doing so, he was also able to make great practical advances as well—indeed, he was one of the first electrical engineers. Heaviside was unique in that he invented new mathematical concepts and equations that had immediate implications in telecommunications, turning long-distance transmissions from a novelty to a functional technology.

WHY DID HE SAY THIS?

Heaviside's quote is in reference to the fact that he had mastered, and put to use, techniques that even he didn't understand. That sounds weird, but perhaps an analogy will shed light on it.

Imagine being the first person to use a screwdriver when everyone else was using a hammer and nails. Moreover, imagine they felt like they *really* understood the principles of hammering nails, and that was the *reason* for them working so well. These people didn't like screwdrivers because they didn't understand them, didn't know how to use them, and hence, didn't trust them. Heaviside didn't bother understanding all the fundamental details that went into the new tools he invented. He didn't have time! He was too busy using them. But, the rest of the scientific community continued to criticize him for it, even when he could clearly demonstrate the utility of his methods.

Heaviside spent most of his life at odds with the scientific community, and he found it difficult to gain recognition for his ideas. His papers were rejected from many journals and magazines because of his unconventional style. The Royal Society rejected one of Heaviside's papers from its proceedings on the grounds that his approach to mathematics was "cavalier." Heaviside's reaction was disbelief, since he could demonstrate his techniques always produced the correct answer.

Today, long after his death, his contributions to electrical engineering, mathematics, and science have been properly understood and recognized.

BE A HEAVISIDE

As you can imagine, Heaviside's quote was said with an air of sarcasm, but it holds an important kernel of truth that has been said many times in many different ways. Let's go with Voltaire, who said, "the best is the enemy of the good." In today's world, there is more pressure than ever to at least display perfection, but we must resist!

Your intuition acts as a guide to new places and ideas. These are the things that interest you and that you feel drawn to. Explore them. Don't worry about whether or not you understand everything—that comes with time and with experience. Besides, even the people who purport to be experts don't really know everything. Their negativity can even be fueled by the insecurity derived from this fact.

To learn how to ignore the naysayers like Heaviside, and forge your own path, follow these tips.

1. START WITH THE TOOLS YOU HAVE.

Don't wait until you have all the tools you need before you start using them. Use the tools you have and learn as you go. This is how Heaviside made such great progress. He didn't wait until he understood everything before he started—he just used what tools he could and figured them out as he went. The tools you have are usually good enough to get the ball rolling. As you go, you'll learn new skills and techniques that you can incorporate into your toolbox.

Heaviside grew up rough and poor and was forced to teach himself mathematics and physics in his spare time while laying telegraph cables and doing electrical work.

During his study, he came across the famous *Treatise on Electricity and Magnetism* by James Clerk Maxwell. He knew it was important, but he did not have the advanced mathematical tools to understand it. He spent years toiling over it until he finally gave up on understanding exactly what Maxwell did and "followed his own course." He invented new methods of mathematics to do so based on his own understanding and eventually rewrote Maxwell's dense mathematical formulas into the four simple but famous equations they are today.

Let's say you are an aspiring musician who wants to learn how to play the guitar. You could take years of lessons and read hundreds of books on music theory before you ever touch the instrument. Or you could just buy a cheap guitar and start playing it. You are keen to start playing right away, so you do just that. You learn some basic chords that allow you to play simple songs. You know that to be a professional musician, taking years of lessons and reading hundreds of books on music theory is probably a good idea. But you are happy to simply play the guitar for fun and let experience be your guide.

2. DON'T WAIT FOR PERFECT.

Heaviside understood that progress is made by taking action and moving forward. If you wait for things to be perfect before you finish them, they'll never get done. Why? Because things are never perfect—they're only good enough. The closer you get to perfection, the more time and energy you'll need to make lesser and lesser progress. At some point, you need to declare that something is good enough and move on.

Heaviside did not have all the mathematical skills

needed to understand everything known about electro-magnetic forces, but he knew enough to make progress by taking action and learning as he went. By doing so, he made great strides in our understanding of these forces.

Suppose you have always dreamed of being a writer—at least, maybe in your spare time. You dream of writing the next great novel, but you have no idea how even to start. You imagine that you need the perfect characters and the perfect plot. But instead, you decide just to write something—anything—and see where it takes you. You are surprised at how quick and painless it was. It's not great, but you finished it. Now, with your first draft complete, you can go back and edit the story without worrying about ruining a plot you once thought was perfect.

3. FOCUS ON THE END GOAL.

Heaviside was able to make great progress because he had a clear end goal in mind—he wanted to make practical advances in the study of electricity and magnetism. This allowed him to focus on the things that were important and ignore the things that weren't. At the time, there were lots of competing theories about the best transmission line methods—and strong opinions to back them up—but rather than refute each of them, Heaviside undertook research in his own home to directly validate his equations.

When you have a clear end goal in mind, it's easier to stay focused and make progress. Don't get bogged down in details that don't matter—because there are a lot of them! Remember that what is proclaimed important is always an opinion. If it is the consensus among experts, you should probably pay attention. But if something is a distraction from achieving your goals, be sure it is actually important before diverting your attention to it.

Imagine you are a runner who wants to run a marathon. You have never done it before, but you are willing to put in the training required. The first thing you need to do is sign up for a race and start training. As part of your training, you learn about things like proper form, how to fuel your body, pacing, and so on. But you are tempted also by lots of other details that don't really matter—like what kind of watch you wear or whether compression socks help performance. You could spend hours researching these topics and reading articles on the internet written by "experts" with strong opinions one way or another. But rather than letting these irrelevant details stress you out, you stick to your focused training. Race day comes, and you end up a proud finisher of a full marathon.

THE SCIENCE

In a discussion around STEM (science, technology, engineering, and mathematics) education to support lifelong learning, Roth and Van Eijck argue that the real world presents very little that looks like school science. In other words, school science, with its emphasis on teaching a breadth of facts and concepts, does not adequately prepare children for the kinds of problematic situations they will face in the world. Instead, they argue, schools should cultivate a particular disposition toward problem solving, which includes something perfectly captured by the French word *débrouillardise*, or *creative resourcefulness*. The ability to cope with the uncertainty of a "learning-as-you-go" attitude is seen as paramount for twenty-first-century skills.

Of course, diving headlong into something you are completely unprepared for, are not confident in, or don't have support to achieve is foolhardy. In the context of work, learning as you go is what is known as on-the-job training. In vastly different job sectors, van der Klink and Streumer found that such methods were useful, but only in conjunction with a positive mindset and managerial support.

It is said that the opposite of perfectionism is acceptance—the attitude that there exists a "good enough." The Pareto principle (or 80/20 rule) says that 80 percent of possible outputs come from 20 percent of the inputs. In other words, you can reach 80 percent perfection with only 20 percent effort. That's not a recommendation to put little effort in but an illustration that, the closer to perfection one strives, the larger the share of effort is required. Ultimately, 100 percent perfection is impossible, and striving for it is dangerous in that it will consume all the energy you have.

Psychologist Thomas Greenspon argues that the popular

notion of "healthy perfectionism" is more properly considered as a strive for excellence rather than the burdensome experience of "dysfunctional perfectionism." In the latter, the sufferer focuses on the experience of their own and other people's expectations. A generic "strive for excellence" is, thus, fine, but perfectionism should be avoided. Indeed the expectations of others can easily become a distraction. In 2015, the average business user sent and received 122 emails *every single day*, and each one likely came with the expectation of a prompt reply.

Digital distractions are bad. While that seems obvious, scientists Kushlev, Proulx, and Dunn have done the studies. Indeed, checking email less frequently reduces daily stress, which in turn contributed to greater well-being. In a separate study, they found that participants with smartphones in sight and notifications turned on throughout the day reported higher levels of inattention. The remedy is simple yet still seems to elude most of us.

Heaviside obviously didn't have digital distractions, but every generation has its vices. The point is to recognize where your distractions lie so you can work to eliminate them and focus on your goal.

"IF I HAVE SEEN FURTHER, IT IS BY STANDING ON THE SHOULDERS OF GIANTS."

—ISAAC NEWTON

WHY LISTEN TO
ISAAC NEWTON?

Isaac Newton was born on Christmas Day in 1642 in England. After a tumultuous childhood, he would eventually become one of the most influential scientists of all time. He made groundbreaking discoveries in mathematics, optics, and physics. In fact, all of premodern physics is known simply as Newtonian physics. Even today, Newton's laws of motion and gravity are used to explain the behavior of objects both on Earth and in space.

WHY DID HE SAY THIS?

The stories told about Newton are stereotypical of a lonesome genius. Yet, even if Newton was a bit reclusive, he did not achieve all that he did by himself—he built on the work of others who came before him. Newton was trained, like all students in England at the time, in the system of Aristotle. But wherever his formal education was lacking, he would supplement it with the works of the latest thinkers, which happened to be the intellectual giants of the Scientific Revolution. On the topic of astronomy, he would read Galileo and Kepler. On philosophy and mathematics, he would read Descartes. These were Newton's giants.

Newton was not shy about acknowledging how he drew from the ideas of others. Newton wrote these words in a letter to Robert Hooke, an English scientist who preceded Newton in many fields

97

of study. Newton wanted to recognize that his accomplishments were based on the intellectual achievements that came before him and built upon them. He gave credit where it was due but didn't submit to the bullying culture that dominated Renaissance science. Indeed, Hooke and Newton ended up as bitter rivals. Though all accounts paint Newton as the modest victor and Hooke as the indignant loser, we will never know the true facts of history.

What is clear is that Newton recognized that he was able to go beyond what he and others could achieve on their own because he had the benefit of the knowledge and wisdom of previous pioneers and groundbreakers. Newton himself then became a giant in his own right. All of physics now stands on his shoulders.

BE A NEWTON

Newton did a lot, but in some sense, there wasn't much to do. The term *Renaissance man* refers to someone who knows a bit about everything. Newton was considered such because he studied the works of nearly everyone worth studying. But, even if you had the time, that's nowhere near possible today, if only because there's just too much to know.

There is a term today that is used for someone with a wide breadth of knowledge that they draw on to solve complex problems—it is a *polymath*. This is an ideal worth striving for, but it must be remembered that the *lonesome genius* is a simplification to reduce the number of characters in the story. No one has, and no one ever will, succeed alone. Tackling the challenges of the world today is an impossible task if undertaken by yourself. However, with the host of challenges and information we are constantly bombarded with, there comes a host of solutions devised by other clever people. These are your giants.

Want to learn how to see further than Newton himself? Follow these three tips.

1. IMPROVE THE WHEEL.

Newton read the works of Galileo and others about designs for telescopes that mostly made use of glass lenses. These had several disadvantages due to the way different colors of light refract, which Newton had a theory for. To get around the problem, he didn't reinvent the telescope but improved upon the design, using reflecting mirrors instead of lenses. It was enough to impress even King Charles II.

The point is don't reinvent the wheel; improve it. There's

no need to start from scratch when there's already a perfectly good solution out there. Take a look at what's been done before and see how you can build on it. Don't just look for solutions in your wheelhouse, either—you can learn a lot by looking at the world through the lens of other disciplines. Most importantly, be humble and give credit where credit is due.

Let's say you are a parent with a fussy eater. You've tried everything from bribing them with dessert to threatening them with no dinner at all, but nothing seems to get those vegetables into their belly. One day, you read an article by someone who has come up with a solution that seems to work: every time their child eats their vegetables, they get one sticker. Once they've collected ten stickers, they can trade them in for a vegetable-free dinner. OK, not bad. But you decide to improve upon it. You add a catch: stickers don't accrue forever. if they don't reach ten stickers by the end of each week, then they have to eat whatever you make for dinner on Sunday night, veggies included. Otherwise, they get to choose Sunday night's dinner. Your system is now more effective because it uses positive reinforcement as well as negative reinforcement. After a few weeks of missing out on their favorite meal, your child decides to play your little game. They cheekily make sure to win ten—and only ten—stickers! In the end, it's a win-win—they get to invoke their agency and you get the peace of mind that at least some vegetables have been eaten.

2. READ THE CLASSICS.

Newton had access to an extensive library, and he was always reading about the latest discoveries. It was quite obvious that he read them, because his scribbles still adorn the pages of many of the over 1,700 books he left behind. It's no wonder he found shoulders to stand on!

How can you stand on the shoulders of giants if you don't know any? The best way to learn from the giants who came before you is to read about their work. Not only will you learn about their ideas, but you'll also get a sense of their thought process and how they approached problems. Of course, you have the ultimate library at your disposal today. So type those names into the search bar and start reading!

Imagine you are a marketing manager for a small clothing company that makes sustainable activewear. You want to create an ad campaign that will really make an impact, but you're struggling to come up with something original. Besides, the whole idea of encouraging consumerism is weighing on your conscience—it's a real crisis! Instead of staring at a blank screen all day, you finally decide to take some inspiration from the greats. You look at Apple's "Think Different" campaign, and Nike's "Just Do It." Sure they're a bit dated, and their companies are not ranked as the most environmentally conscious, but some things never change. Through studying these campaigns you realize that what you have in common is counterculture. "Green is the New Black." It's perfect. It resonates with your existing customers and sends a message that is core to your ethos.

3. FIND A MENTOR.

When Newton enrolled at Cambridge University, the standard mathematics curriculum was based primarily on classical Greek geometry. Newton's mathematics professor,

Isaac Barrow, recognized his ability and steered him toward studying more advanced subjects, including the connection between physics and mathematics. This ultimately led to Newton's famed invention of calculus. It was Barrow who brought it to the attention of the wider mathematics community and secured Newton a professorship at Cambridge.

A mentor is someone who has already achieved what you want to achieve and can help guide you to success. Find someone you respect and can learn from. Don't be afraid to ask for help when you need it. There's no shame in admitting that you need assistance. In fact, it's a sign of strength.

Suppose you've finally decided to leave the corporate world and just landed your dream job as a product manager at a small start-up. You are excited to start working and building cool things, but on your first day, you realize that you have no idea what you're doing. Everyone else seems to know what they're doing and moves around the office with purpose. You feel lost and alone. Luckily, the cofounder has been through the exact same thing before and is happy to offer support. You meet regularly over coffee, and they give you useful tips on how to work in a small team and how the start-up mentality differs from corporate culture. Before you know it, you are cruising around the office with confidence. When you notice a new face at reception with a familiar lost look, you immediately know what to do.

THE SCIENCE

Open any scientific journal, and the phrase "building on the work of others" is bound to appear in one of the articles. This admission embodies the idiom "don't reinvent the wheel." But what about outside of purely scientific pursuits?

In his book *Laws of UX: Using Psychology to Design Better Products & Services*, Jon Yablonski recounts "Jakob's Law of Internet User Experience": "Users spend most of their time on other sites, and they prefer your site to work the same way as all the other sites they already know." In other words, if you are making a product or delivering a service, don't reinvent the wheel for the simple reason that users have expectations. Build on the success of what works.

Appe and Schnable have demonstrated that grassroots nongovernment organizations (NGOs) suffer greatly from reinventing the wheel due to their reliance on volunteers without professional experience. They argue that the nearly 10,000 grassroots NGOs could benefit from support organizations with experience that can be built upon.

In Bloom's famous *Taxonomy of Educational Objectives*, the cognitive domain is broken into a hierarchical pyramid with foundational knowledge at its base. In this model of learning, the basics—upon which all learning is built—are dependent on the field of study. If you are studying human biology, you'll need to be able to recognize and remember parts of the body and their basic functionality. If you are a computer coder, you'll need to have memorized the syntax and specifications of various programming languages. If you want to be a literary critic, you'll need to literally *read the classics*. Whatever the topic you want to understand, there'll be basic concepts you'll need to be familiar with.

In the context of medical training, health education

professionals in the Netherlands overviewed the landscape of mentorship programs in medical education. While studies show the benefits of mentorship, including productivity, job satisfaction, and career progression, they noted that less than half of medical residents in some institutions have mentors. The obvious conclusion was a recommendation for formal mentoring programs, which may include guidance on finding a suitable mentor in the first place.

Importantly, the mentor–mentee relationship and its benefits are not one-way. Across a wide variety of disciplines, researchers have found that *mentors* enjoy improved performance and job satisfaction as short-term side effects of both formal and informal mentoring relationships.

By standing on the shoulders of giants, you will be able to see further than you ever could have on your own. And remember that you, too, are a giant. Help others achieve their goals and reach their potential.

"AN ADMISSION OF IGNORANCE MAY WELL BE A STEP TO A NEW DISCOVERY."

—CECILIA PAYNE-GAPOSCHKIN

WHY LISTEN TO
CECILIA PAYNE-GAPOSCHKIN?

Cecilia Payne-Gaposchkin was a twentieth-century astrophysicist who made groundbreaking discoveries about the composition of stars. In particular, she showed that stars are mostly made of hydrogen and helium. This was a revolutionary idea at the time, as most scientists believed that stars were made of the same stuff as the Earth—which is patently not a fiery ball of only two inert gasses. In fact, the idea was *too* revolutionary and was initially rejected. Payne-Gaposchkin's work overturned the prevailing wisdom, and she is now considered one of the most important astronomers of all time.

WHY DID SHE SAY THIS?

Admitting your mistakes is often seen as a weakness. If you're in a position of authority and admit that you made a mistake, you may feel that you've undermined your credibility. Surrounded by many important scientists, Payne-Gaposchkin could see this reluctance at play. She could clearly see that fame and power were primarily a burden for a devoted scientist. That thirst for knowledge and understanding is only sated through the application of intellectual integrity.

It was as a student working on her first research problem that she let her pride get the best of her. Her adviser directed her to solve a set of equations. She could have admitted then that she did not know how to solve them, but she didn't. In the end, she did solve them, but only after enduring the challenge of reading five enormous volumes of mathematics books written in a different language. Payne-Gaposchkin recalled this episode in her autobiography as the pivotal moment that awakened her intellectual integrity. In fact, her quote is in reference to this anecdote.

While she may have been referring to an admission of ignorance to her adviser in this example, which would have saved her many hours of work, the deeper lesson was about realizing and owning her limitations. It's a lesson that has served her well throughout her life and career. Fame and position can be acquired by several means that should be resisted. Payne-Gaposchkin did so by constantly questioning herself and her ideas. She was not afraid to admit when she was wrong, and embracing that is what led to her ultimate success.

BE A PAYNE-GAPOSCHKIN

Admitting you messed up is hard to do, but taking responsibility for your actions by owning them can sometimes make all the difference. Apologizing is also a form of self-care, as it can eliminate some of the guilt and shame you may be feeling. It shows that you are constantly improving, which is a major trait in an emotionally intelligent person.

This is a lesson that we can all learn from. We live in a world where it's easy to be confident and sure of ourselves. It's too easy to find information that might confirm our existing biases. But this will lead only to stagnation.

Here are three tips on embracing your ignorance that might bring you closer to your next big leap forward.

1. QUESTION EVERYTHING.

Payne-Gaposchkin's greatest discovery came about because she questioned the prevailing wisdom. That stars are made of hydrogen is a fact told to children today—so simple! But it was Payne-Gaposchkin's question that led to it. Her initial observations were, of course, not conclusive, and they flew in the face of the consensus of the scientific community, which was that stars were made of the same stuff as found on Earth. But what if that was wrong—what if stars were fundamentally different? Well, that would be a revolution. Of course, Payne-Gaposchkin's PhD thesis concluded it more tactfully than that—yet it was a revolution in astronomy.

Just because something is the way it is, doesn't mean it has to stay that way. Don't be afraid to challenge assumptions and ask tough questions. Oftentimes, it is the question that should be credited for a great discovery, not the solution. A profound question might have a simple solution, but without the question, there is no solution.

Suppose you are brought into a new team as a sales manager to help with performance, which is well below what is expected. You analyze the data to see what might be causing it, but you don't find anything obvious. It's time to start asking deeper questions. Is it possible that the entire sales process is flawed? That seems unlikely, but you investigate and discover that it is. It turns out that the sales process was inherited from the company the team was acquired from...in a different market! Once you realize this, it becomes clear that, to increase sales, the process must be changed. Asking the tough questions has led you to a major breakthrough.

2. BE COMFORTABLE WITH UNCERTAINTY.

Payne-Gaposchkin was comfortable with not having all the answers. In fact, it was her willingness to entertain uncertainty that led her down untrodden paths. If she had been afraid of failure, she might never have made any breakthroughs. In fact, she was dissuaded by very prominent astronomers of the time not to make such brazen claims against the orthodoxy—yet, she persisted in the face of doubt and uncertainty.

There is no such thing as a sure thing. Anytime you embark on a new venture, you are taking a risk. Be prepared for the possibility of failure. Embrace uncertainty and use it to your advantage. Not everyone enjoys, or can even handle, change, which presents an opportunity to capitalize on unexplored ideas. Successful people

are often those who are willing to take risks and embrace uncertainty. They don't let the fear of failure stop them from pursuing their goals.

Let's say you have a steady job but are an entrepreneur at heart. You also happen to have a new start-up idea. You are passionate about your product, and you strongly believe in its potential, but there is always the risk that it might not take off as you expect. What do you do? One option would be to play it safe—stay in the steady job and work on your new business idea on the side. The other option would be to go all in—quit your job and put every-thing into the business. This is obviously much riskier, but if things go well, then you will have achieved something great. You also realize that the strategy of playing it safe and taking years to bring your product to market will fail while you keep your day job. Ultimately, you know you are prepared for the risks, and so you start to write your resignation letter.

3. LEARN FROM YOUR MISTAKES.

Payne-Gaposchkin's success came about because she was constantly learning and evolving. She didn't just avoid making the same mistakes—she changed her entire way of thinking. And that is what led to her groundbreaking discoveries.

Nobody is perfect. We all make mistakes. The key is to learn from them. It should be easy to simply not repeat the same mistake in the future. But what is harder is to make a change in your pattern of thinking. Sometimes the lessons are hard, like the one Payne-Gaposchkin learned about admitting her ignorance, but these can help define us as stronger, more resilient, and intelligent people.

Imagine you are starting a new job. You work hard and do everything you can to impress your boss and colleagues. But one day, you make a mistake that causes an important client to be very angry. Your boss is not happy, either. What do you do? The easy way out would be to try to cover up the mistake or blame someone else. You realize that would only make things worse in the long run if it were discovered (which it most likely would be). It's much better to take responsibility for what happened—admit that you made a mistake and offer a solution for how to fix it. By doing this, you've shown that you are willing to learn from your mistakes instead of repeating them. Not only do you help defuse the situation, but also both your boss and the client appreciate the level of maturity you've shown.

THE SCIENCE

They say ignorance is bliss, but what they meant was humility is salvation. But this is difficult even in the (presumably) most humble of human activities—science—which prides itself on self-correction...or does it? Recent evidence suggests this is not always the case, as a variety of factors act as competing interests. What this underscores is that admitting ignorance is hard!

After admitting ignorance, the first step is resolving it. To do so, we ask questions. What counts as a *good* question is still up for debate. Even in areas such as *computational linguistics*, where researchers try to teach machines to ask "good" questions, there is no consensus. Interestingly, a team of researchers from New York University found that, in an experimental setting where the best question was known, *real* people could accurately evaluate questions presented to them but rarely came up with the "best" question themselves. All this suggests that learning to ask good questions is hard!

In his book *A More Beautiful Question*, Warren Berger points to several success stories that started with what-if questions. These at times wildly hypothetical questions have a yet-to-be-measured creative spark that has been identified over and over and repackaged in many forms. In *Tools of Titans*, Tim Ferriss interviewed successful people in the tech sector and found a common theme: successful people ask a lot of what they admit are "dumb" questions. It seems there's nothing to lose in asking questions—whether they are deeply profound or dirt simple, ask away.

Reporting in *Advances in Health Sciences Education*, a team of health education professionals reviewed the various strategies for achieving "comfort with uncertainty" in the high-stakes and high-stress field of clinical diagnoses. They found that those with a flexible plan of treatment displayed the most confidence in the actions they took. In other words, conscious recognition of uncertainty led to adaptive behaviors ideally suited for resolving complex and evolving situations. Moreover, these traits are honed by experience, suggesting that such mental fortitude can be learned and practiced.

Neuroscience shows that learning from mistakes is natural and, for many simple tasks, unconsciously automatic. Researchers found that we learn faster when we initially make poor predictions, albeit in a controlled experimental setting. What about more complex scenarios? Again in the context of training medical professionals, where mistakes are potentially fatal, the situation is more nuanced. Researchers from the University of Massachusetts Chan Medical School found that trainees learned best when harm was caused during mistakes. In any situation, however, the key to learning from mistakes is *feedback*—you can't learn from a mistake if you don't know you've made one! In other words, seek feedback early and often, and be ready to correct your errors.

Ignorance can be a good thing if you use it as an opportunity to learn and grow. Be like Payne-Gaposchkin, and don't let your preconceptions hold you back from greatness.

"ALL OUT-STANDING WORK RESULTS FROM...

IMMENSE ZEAL APPLIED TO A GREAT IDEA."

—SANTIAGO RAMÓN Y CAJAL

WHY LISTEN TO **SANTIAGO RAMÓN Y CAJAL?**

Santiago Ramón y Cajal was born in a small Spanish town in the mid-nineteenth century. He is considered one of the pioneers of modern neuroscience, specializing in neuroanatomy. He is often credited for elucidating our modern conception of the brain. He shared the 1906 Nobel Prize in Medicine for his work on the structure of the central nervous system. His meticulous drawings of neurons are still used today for training students in biology and medicine.

WHY DID HE SAY THIS?

Dendritic spines look like tiny hairs protruding from the branches of nerve cells. They were seen before Ramón y Cajal entered the scene but were thought to be an artifact of the staining method, which allowed the cells to be seen under a microscope. Ramón y Cajal became obsessed with spines not only because he thought they were real but also because he understood them to be critically important to synaptic connections in the brain.

Ramón y Cajal was so passionate about neuroscience that he worked on it until his death at the age of eighty-two. A shaky handwritten letter was received by a colleague only two days before his death urging the young protégé to continue his work on spines. It is for this reason that Ramón y Cajal himself credited his scientific successes to his willpower applied to good techniques rather than to his intelligence or education, and especially not to his pedigree.

Unlike many quotable quips from famous people, Ramón y Cajal's quote was not taken out of context but stated plainly in his book titled *Advice for a Young Investigator*. Indeed, he preached what he practiced because, unlike many scientists, he was also passionate about educating young or novice scientists about the best attitude to even approach the subject.

Ramón y Cajal said that this advice was aimed at the "spirit" more than the intellect, and he was one of the few who thought this possible or even worthwhile.

BE A RAMÓN Y CAJAL

Ramón y Cajal's advice applies to every type of creative pursuit, from painting and writing to cooking and designing. Pursuits like these often seem easy at first glance—but if you dig a little deeper, it quickly becomes clear that they require a lot of hard work in order to be truly successful. Find your passion and put in the work. Be meticulous about what you do, and never give up on an idea that gets you excited.

Sometimes it can feel a bit overwhelming to try and tackle something new. But if you have a great idea that gets you excited, it's worth putting in the extra effort to see it through. Ramón y Cajal may not have been the smartest person in his field, but he had an unshakable passion for neuroscience—and that made all the difference.

To jump-start a passion for your own project, follow these three tips.

1. SET ASIDE TIME FOR LEARNING.

In his advice to enterprising young investigators, Ramón y Cajal stressed the avoidance of unnecessary distractions, which would have been different in his day, but ultimately had the same effect of stolen time. Time and concentration were, to him, the currency of not only deep understanding but the necessary toll to achieve mastery.

One of the biggest obstacles to learning something new is finding the time to do it. We are all busy with our work, family, and social lives, and it can be difficult to find extra time in our schedules. But if you want to learn something new, you need to make time for it.

As an example, suppose you are a busy working

professional who wants to learn how to cook. You may not have a lot of extra time during the week, but you can probably find an hour or two on the weekends. So you set aside some time each weekend to experiment in the kitchen. You start by watching cooking shows, reading recipes, and trying out new dishes. You make mistakes—but you learn from them, and gradually you become an excellent cook. Unfortunately, now every dinner party happens at your place!

2. GET EXCITED.

Ramón y Cajal was a rebellious child—even spending time in prison as an eleven-year-old for destroying his neighbor's property with a homemade cannon! His father tried forcing many mundane jobs on him for a sense of stability, but nothing stuck. One day, his father—who was

a surgeon and medical teacher—took him to a graveyard to study the anatomy of bones. Ramón y Cajal sketched some of the bones and found the exercise so fascinating that it motivated him to enroll in medical school. He never looked back.

Of course, not everyone will find—or even has—a life-long passion before adulthood. But you can't just sit back and passively consume information hoping for something to excite you—take an active approach to learn by actively seeking out new experiences. Get involved in as many different activities as possible so that you can gain first-hand knowledge about various topics and issues. And when you come across something that interests you, don't hesitate to dive deep and explore it further.

Imagine you are a high school student who is trying to decide what to do with your life. You might start by taking some aptitude tests to see what you're good at and then research various career paths that interest you. But eventually, you need to take the plunge and actually try out some of these careers for yourself. You like the idea of teaching, so you decide to volunteer at an elementary school. You find that you love the challenge and reward of working with young kids who need extra support. So, you decide to take a vocational training course to be a school support worker.

3. START SMALL AND BUILD UP SLOWLY.

Ramón y Cajal also recommended taking things slow in order to avoid getting overwhelmed or discouraged. When he was starting out as a scientist, he didn't try to tackle big problems right away. Instead, he focused on smaller tasks that allowed him to gradually increase his knowledge base. Over time, this approach helped him develop into one of the world's leading neuroscientists—even though he admitted he wasn't the smartest person in his field.

This same advice can be applied to any creative pursuit: Don't try to do too much at once or take on projects that are too complex for your current skill level—instead, start small and build up slowly over time. It can be tempting to immediately jump into something new and exciting when starting out on a creative journey. But it's important to be patient and give yourself time to learn the ropes before taking on anything too challenging. Start small and focus on gradually increasing your skills so that you can eventually tackle bigger projects down the line.

Let's say you're interested in painting. Instead of deciding up front that you are going to do cubism with oil on canvas, you start by experimenting with different mediums and styles. You move back and forth between them on small projects until you find a particular method or genre that you feel the best about. Then, you focus on mastering the basics of that particular technique before moving on to more complex techniques. You don't worry about your early attempts, which are not as good as you would like them to be, because you know that creativity is often about trial and error. The key, you know, is to keep practicing and learning from your mistakes so that you can gradually improve over time. After a while, when you look back at where you started, you realize that you could have never imagined you were capable of great artistic creations.

THE SCIENCE

Non-Western concepts are often derided as mysticism, but the tides are turning in the area of international well-being research. Traditionally, such topics focused on the subjective happiness or quality of life of study subjects. However, contemporary research has begun to embrace a broader notion of well-being. Most relevant to the quote from Ramón y Cajal is the Japanese concept of *ikigai*. While no complete and direct translation to English is possible, it roughly means "reason for being." Rather than the *quality* of life, this notion focuses on the *purpose* of life. Psychologist Michiko Kumano has studied *ikigai* inasmuch as it entails a devotion to enjoyable pursuits resulting in feelings of accomplishment of meaningful goals, noting that this doesn't necessarily correlate with happiness as traditionally understood in Western literature.

Time and capacity are important, as evidenced by the fact that among the Japanese elderly, *ikigai* is generally lost after retirement. In response, the government created an initiative to provide part-time work for the elderly, which increased *ikigai*. Finding the time and creating opportunities to focus on what is meaningful to you personally is essential for well-being.

Ramón y Cajal's story is, of course, simplified. His passion developed over many years rather than instantly by "discovery." In Japan, *ikigai* is intimately linked with education. While young students are forming the concept, they draw heavily from parents, teachers, and community leaders. Into adulthood, a cycle forms beginning with the identification of a topic of interest, followed by study and practice, and the accumulation of life experiences, which eventually lead to new interests, renewing the cycle.

A team of psychologists found that participants who thought that personal interests were a fixed thing to be found, rather than developed, expected that boundless motivation would make tasks easy. Moreover, when the tasks turned out not to be easy, these participants quickly gave up. In other words, a passion should be thought of not as something to be found but as something to be grown.

Westernized versions of *ikigai* are closest to the concept of *flow* introduced by Mihaly Csikszentmihalyi, which is the state of mind sometimes referred to as being "in the zone." You are said to have achieved flow if you are putting in "voluntary effort to accomplish something difficult and worthwhile." Various scales, such as the Flow State Scale, have been introduced in an attempt to measure these qualities.

The most straightforward explanatory variables are the challenge of a task and the skill level currently possessed. If a task is easy, then regardless of skill, the mental state is typically some variant of boredom. If the task is difficult and the level of skill of the person is low, then their mental state will likely be some form of anxiety. The flow state is when a highly skilled person is performing a challenging task. But skills, as you know, take time and dedicated practice to develop.

There are no shortcuts when it comes to obtaining a life of meaning. As Ramón y Cajal said, you have to put in the effort if you want results!

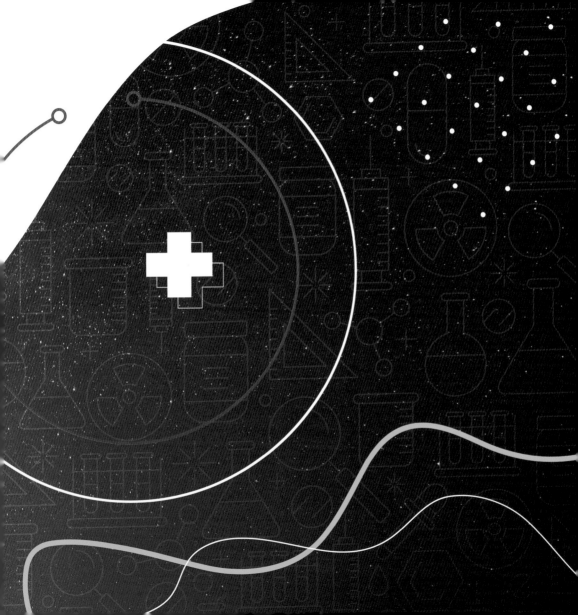

"LOVE OF LEARNING IS THE MOST NECESSARY PASSION…

IN IT LIES OUR HAPPINESS. IT'S A SURE REMEDY FOR WHAT AILS US,

AN UNENDING SOURCE OF PLEASURE. "

—ÉMILIE DU CHÂTELET

WHY LISTEN TO
ÉMILIE DU CHÂTELET?

Gabrielle Émilie Le Tonnelier de Breteuil, Marquise du Châtelet, was born into a French noble family in 1706 during a time of great prosperity. She was a highly educated woman who was fluent in six languages, including Latin, Greek, Italian, German, English, and, of course, her native French. As such, she was an important translator of many works of philosophy, science, and mathematics. Her translation of Isaac Newton's *Principia* into French remains the standard translation to this day. Her contributions to the fields of physics and mathematics mark her as one of the most influential intellectuals of the French Enlightenment.

WHY DID SHE SAY THIS?

If you've ever *had* to read Newton's original version of his *Principia*, you'd wonder why anyone would do so willingly. Indeed, it is likely that only a few physicists alive today have even looked at the first page—and even then, they are probably historians compelled to do so. Du Châtelet was a marquise, a woman of high social rank, which came with expectations and various affordances that would not have necessitated the study of natural philosophy. But she was wildly curious and excelled at using her many talents to engage in the world around her rather than perform the expected responsibilities of a woman at that time.

At a young age, she was deterred by her mother from pursuing her intellectual curiosity as women were not normally part of public intellectual life in France (or anywhere in the world, for that matter). She was married to another noble and bore three children by the age of twenty-six. She considered her marital duties fulfilled and struck a deal with her husband to lead separate lives. Du Châtelet turned back to education, seeking tutelage from the greatest mathematicians of the day.

Du Châtelet was an unwavering advocate for the importance of education, particularly for women. She believed that education was necessary for both men and women in order to participate fully in society. Du Châtelet also argued that women should not be limited to learning only those things that were considered to be appropriate for their gender. She believed that women should be able to study any subject they were interested in. She blazed this trail even when it required disguising herself in men's clothing to engage in intellectual discussions and debate.

Duties, expectations, pain, boredom—whatever it may have been, du Châtelet always had learning to fall back on to cure those ails. She never felt her education was complete and even raced toward maximizing it as her death approached—for she knew that, as a pregnant woman over forty, she was unlikely to survive the birth. She completed a commentary of Newton's work a day before giving birth. She died six days later—a tragic end to a vivacious life still full of potential.

BE A DU CHÂTELET

In the mid-eighteenth century, du Châtelet, being a highly intelligent woman, knew she would not survive childbirth, even confiding it to a friend in a letter. Today, death in childbirth is extremely uncommon in developed nations. Indeed, progress over the centuries has been marked by a rapid increase in the overall quality and longevity of life. Yet, at the same time, you can walk into any bookstore to find that the most popular nonfiction genre is self-help (witness you reading this book now). For all the modern world has given us, we still want to know how to be happy. Perhaps the answer is as easy as du Châtelet recommends.

To learn to love learning, try these three tips.

1. FOLLOW YOUR CURIOSITY.

Du Châtelet was curious about everything from the stars to fashion. She was not afraid to learn new things, even if it meant disguise and deception. In today's world, you can openly engage in intellectual curiosity without fear of repercussions (at least in most developed nations). So take advantage of that freedom!

The root of all learning is curiosity. It's the driving force that compels us to ask questions and find answers. When you have a question, Google it. When you see something interesting, look it up. Be curious about the world around you and learn as much as you can about everything that piques your interest—even if it seems like pointless trivia at first glance. You never know when that knowledge will come in handy or be just plain fascinating.

As an example, suppose you are a fan of the band U2. You might be curious about how they got their start, what influences their music, or why they are one of the most successful bands in history. So you do some research and find out that lead singer Bono was born Paul David Hewson in Dublin, Ireland, on May 10, 1960. He started a rock band called Feedback with his friends at Mount Temple Comprehensive School when he was fourteen years old. The band changed its name to The Hype and then finally settled on U2 after a friend suggested it as simple and ambiguous. It definitely wasn't a pun on "you too" or a reference to the spy plane by the same name. Is that important knowledge? Who knows? Maybe this will give you a greater appreciation for their music or just help you at the next trivia night. Either way, it definitely didn't hurt you.

2. LEARN FOR LEARNING'S SAKE.

In her time, du Châtelet had to fight for the right to be educated. It wasn't easy being one of the few highly educated women in her day, but du Châtelet persisted because she loved learning for its own sake. For du Châtelet, learning was not only its own reward but also an escape from the mundane realities of her everyday life. She was not interested in learning only the things that were considered appropriate for a woman at the time—she wanted to learn everything she could about anything and everything that piqued her interest, whether it was literature or physics.

Today, education is more accessible than ever before—there are free online courses offered by some of the best universities in the world on a variety of topics. You no longer need expensive textbooks; all you need is an internet connection and a willingness to learn something new. Learning should be enjoyable, not a chore or a means to an end (although it can help further your career).

Suppose you are enrolled in a university degree you think will lead to a good job but find yourself struggling with schoolwork. You ask yourself whether you would still be doing it if there were no external rewards involved—such as good grades or money. In this case, the answer is yes. You find the material fascinating and want to learn more regardless of the outcome. This thought invigorates you, and you find it much easier to engage with the material and do well in your courses. While it might not lead to the job you expected, you are happy to have broadened your understanding of the world and developed a thirst for knowledge that will guide you through and beyond your next personal adventure.

3. FIND A COMMUNITY OF LEARNERS.

In her day, du Châtelet found a community of like-minded individuals with whom she could engage in intellectual discussion and debate (even if it meant dressing up as a man to do so). These relationships were vital to her development as a thinker and scientist. Today, you can find online communities dedicated to nearly any topic you can think of—whether it's your favorite TV show or hobby, there is likely a group of people out there who share your interest.

When finding or building these communities, look for three things: respectfulness, diverse perspectives, and shared interests. A respectful community is one where people feel safe sharing their thoughts and opinions without fear of ridicule or attack; this creates an environment in which everyone can learn from each other. A community with diverse perspectives helps create interesting discussions because different people bring different experiences and knowledge to the table.

Let's say you are interested in the environment and want to find a community of like-minded individuals. You search online and find an environmental group that meets once a month. At the first meeting, you are surprised to find that not everyone shares your view on the issue—in fact, some people seem to be there just to voice their opposition. However, the group is respectful toward one another, and you learn a lot from hearing different perspectives on the issue. Over time, you develop relationships with some of the members and feel more comfortable sharing your own thoughts and opinions.

THE SCIENCE

A recent review commissioned by UNESCO found evidence that a culture of lifelong learning has the potential to promote global equality, peace, and prosperity, going as far as to argue that it should count as a new human right. Core to their argument was the need to build resilience to today's pace of change and the increasing complexity of challenges faced by global nations and persons. That this is possible through lifelong learning is evidenced primarily by the recent overthrowing of the concept that the human brain is amenable to learning only in youth.

The brain's continual change in response to our environment is known as *neuroplasticity*. Since the early 2000s, our knowledge of this has grown, thanks to the capabilities of advanced neuro-imaging. Brain plasticity is the mechanism through which we can continue to learn throughout our lives. And learn you should, regardless of your age!

A study by the University of Michigan showed that dementia in people over sixty-five fell significantly between the years 2000 and 2012, with a majority contributing factor being the length of formal education. Of course, education does not need to be obtained only from colleges and universities. Continual learning can come from a variety of sources, including vocational training, independent study, and simple reflection on personal life experiences. Another study in the *Oxford Review of Education* found that a love of learning begets confidence and a greater sense of purpose. The participants explained that continual challenges helped them discover new passions and goals.

Bickford and Wright define a community as "a group of people with a common purpose, shared values, and agreement on goals" and review the research on the numerous benefits of such membership in the context of learning. West and Williams point out that learning communities can be defined by various parameters, including access, relationship, vision, and function. Each may have its own set of rewards for membership, but from an individual perspective, you must decide what is most important to you.

It can take some effort to identify, but if you follow du Châtelet and cultivate a love of learning, you may lead a richer, more fulfilling, and satisfying life.

"THERE IS NO LAW EXCEPT THE LAW THAT THERE IS NO LAW."

—JOHN ARCHIBALD WHEELER

WHY LISTEN TO
JOHN ARCHIBALD WHEELER?

John Archibald Wheeler was an American physicist and a rare breed of scientist, having worked on both of the major branches of modern physics: general relativity and quantum theory. He invented the idea of space as a seething boil of virtual particles popping in and out of existence, which has been popularized in blockbuster superhero movies under the name the *quantum realm*. He also coined the terms *wormhole* and *black hole*. He was an influential teacher, supervising fifty physicist PhD students, two of whom went on to win Nobel Prizes.

WHY DID HE SAY THIS?

Wheeler followed his curiosity and insights to the fringes of known physics long before it was mainstream. Many of his ideas did not earn favor from his colleagues for decades, and some were only appreciated after his death. But that did not deter his craving to understand the fundamental nature of reality.

Wheeler was not known for producing a large body of original research, because he placed the utmost priority on teaching and training students, where his favorite technique was asking difficult and often profound questions. One line of thought led him to the idea that theories of physics suggest there is no predetermined reality but, moreover, that our actions bring about reality through the choices we make. We live in a *participatory* universe.

As a physicist, a "law" to Wheeler was any observed regularity or pattern in nature. He realized that these apparent laws could be just a product of the way we observe and think about reality rather than an inherent feature of reality itself. This line of reason has one ultimate conclusion: there are no real laws of nature but those we artificially impose upon it.

BE A WHEELER

Do you ever feel like every good idea has already been taken or that everything worth doing has already been done? Progress in today's world happens so rapidly that it is impossible to keep up with even the latest news and celebrity gossip, let alone new ideas, inventions, and discoveries. For example, Twitter users pump out 650 million tweets per day. Some of those might contain important information, but clearly, you can't follow everyone. So what can you do? Be more like Wheeler.

Step back and think about the fundamentals of your problem. What are the guiding principles you *think* you should be following—that is, what are the laws? Ask yourself if those are necessary and what lies beyond the boundaries set by convention. By constantly challenging yourself to find new answers to old questions, you can open up a world of possibilities. The reality you experience is dictated by your actions and the questions you ask.

Are you ready to take up the torch and venture into the unknown? Then you'll need a few tips.

1. THINK OUTSIDE THE BOX.

For Wheeler, *laws* were the rigid constraints preventing new lines of thought. Laws say which ideas and concepts are meant to be forbidden. They define the proverbial box, which most people feel comfortable thinking in. Wheeler was one of the few scientists who saw past the confines of the "box," and it allowed him to make some of the most significant insights in modern physics.

To think outside the box, you need to be willing to explore all possibilities, no matter how crazy they might seem at first. Be open to new and unorthodox ideas, and don't be afraid to challenge the status quo. You need to recognize when you are constraining your own thoughts by adhering too closely to laws and rules. Once you have identified these moments, take a step back and consider alternatives that might lead to more creative solutions.

Imagine you are a business owner. The recession has hit your business hard, and you're struggling to stay afloat. What do you do? Well, if you're like most people, you cut back on expenses, lay off some employees, and try to increase revenue by selling more products or services. Now imagine that, instead of doing all of that, you decide to give away your products or services for free. That's right, FREE! You might think this is crazy, but it just might work. After all, if people are struggling to pay their bills, they might be more likely to take advantage of a free offer. And if they like what they get, they might be more likely to become paying customers in the future.

2. FOLLOW YOUR INTUITION.

Wheeler had a strong belief in the power of intuition, and he followed his hunches, even when they led him down unexpected paths. Wheeler's ideas were not always well-received by the scientific community. But this willingness to take risks led him to some of his most important discoveries.

Follow your intuition, even when it leads you astray, and you just might find yourself on the path to a breakthrough discovery, whether it is a new idea in theoretical physics or something important you didn't know about yourself. If you always play it safe, you will never know what could have been.

Suppose you are in a rut—bored, uninspired, and rightfully considering whether to take a new job. Your intuition tells you to go for it, even though the salary is lower than you'd like and the commute is longer. By staying, you will be playing it safe with an income and time commitment you are comfortable managing. But...you can't shake that gut instinct. You end up following your intuition and taking the new job. It turns out to be a great decision: you love the work, the people, and the company. By following your intuition, you have found a job that is much more fulfilling than anything else you've ever done.

3. BE PREPARED TO BE WRONG.

Wheeler was constantly revising his ideas in the light of new evidence and new insights. He was not afraid to change his mind, even on fundamental issues. He knew he had to, if he were to explore ideas well beyond the status quo. This openness to being wrong led him to a greater understanding of the universe.

If you want to have original ideas, you need to be prepared for the fact that some of them will be wrong. In fact, you should expect to be wrong most of the time. The key is to learn from your mistakes and use them to refine your thinking.

Let's say you are a musician, and you've just released your first single. You are confident in your work and sure that it will be a hit. But the reviews come back, and they are not as good as you had hoped. Your heart sinks as you read the criticism. It turns out you were wrong about the message that would resonate with your audience. At this point, you could give up and never write another song again, or you could use the feedback to improve your craft and come back stronger than ever with your next release. You choose the latter option, and the critics take notice of your dedication and hard work. In fact, their insights helped you connect more strongly with your audience.

THE SCIENCE

The phrases "off the beaten path" and "outside the box thinking" are related to the psychological concept of *functional fixedness,* which is a cognitive bias limiting the use of objects to the way traditionally used. For example, a full cup of coffee was not designed to be a paperweight but can act as one in a pinch. Someone who would not consider this option suffers from functional fixedness. Evidence suggests that we learn this tendency quite early in life. But this also means that very young children are naturally "outside the box" thinkers.

In almost any discipline you can think of, there exists a review article—with the phrase "thinking outside the box" in the title—compiling lists of resources that focus on education beyond traditional confines. Woods and Rosenberg identify many techniques in areas of conventionally classroom-based instruction. For example, in schools there are flipped classrooms, virtual classrooms, online open classrooms, and so on. For whatever domain you are in, someone has come up with at least one idea to help you think outside the box.

Neuroscience has revealed that many decisions we make are

done so without consciously being aware of them. In animals without apparent consciousness, we often call this "instinct," which is to be contrasted, perhaps a little too audaciously, with the rational decision-making of *Homo sapiens*. (*Sapiens* is a Latin word meaning "one who knows," by the way.) Thus we often elevate so-called rational thinking to lofty goals. However, studies of patients with damage to certain parts of the brain associated with the regulation of emotions found that such damage can make them *more* rational. However, the loss of quick emotion-based decision-making made them less functional overall. After all, life is not a series of rational tests but a nonlinear path of complex interactions that, more often than not, require intuitive judgments.

Of course, the opposite can be true if coupled with overconfidence, which is related to the infamous *Dunning-Kruger effect*. That is, errors based on intuition are much more severe when the person is overconfident in their ability. How can you avoid this?

Well, that is obvious—don't be overconfident. If you make intuitive judgments, you must be prepared that many will be in error, and that's okay if you are humble about it.

By following Wheeler, you can become a better thinker and a more creative problem solver, and you just might make a few discoveries of your own.

"IT'S EASIER TO ASK FORGIVENESS THAN IT IS TO GET PERMISSION."

—GRACE HOPPER

WHY LISTEN TO
GRACE HOPPER?

Grace Hopper was an American computer scientist, United States Navy rear admiral, and one of the first programmers of the Harvard Mark I computer. She popularized the term "debugging" for fixing computer glitches after finding a moth trapped in a relay of the Mark II computer at Harvard University. She also helped develop the first *compiler*, which translated code written in human-understandable language into machine code. Hopper was a pioneer of computer programming abstraction and automation.

WHY DID SHE SAY THIS?

Though she was raised to be hardworking and self-reliant, Hopper is said to have been a curious troublemaker in her youth. She excelled in academic study, obtaining a PhD in mathematics from Yale at the age of twenty-seven. She worked as a professor of mathematics at Vassar College for over ten years until America entered World War II. Hopper was denied military service on account of her age. Undeterred, she applied for a waiver and joined the Naval Reserve.

Hopper's quote captures both of her personality traits—tenacity and defiance. Hopper was a problem solver, a *doer*. Her advice to young people who worried about whether or not something could be done was always, "do it." She would follow up with her students and mentees periodically in life to make sure they

179

were still taking risks. Her defiance was not something she kept secret—she famously flew a prominent Jolly Roger flag in her Navy office.

Hopper was a military officer in one of the largest organizations in the world. The amount of bureaucracy would have been stifling for someone with a desire to enact change. Hopper quickly saw firsthand how red tape can bog down progress. She would tell people within the military never to accept rejection because there was always another way around it.

Importantly, behind what might seem like an indifferent attitude, Hopper's philosophy was to enact change for the greater good. She was not suggesting one do things just because it feels good or has some immediate personal reward. Her implicit advice was that, in the face of arbitrary obstacles, just forge ahead in spite of them to do what you know is right and will help others.

BE A HOPPER

In many organizations today, there are rules and procedures in place to minimize risk and protect against liability. But these same rules can also stifle creativity and prevent people from taking initiative. If you want to be an innovative thinker like Hopper, you need to learn how to work within—or around—bureaucratic systems without letting them grind your ideas to a halt.

In order for something new or different to happen, someone has to take initiative and demonstrate that it can be done—especially if it goes against conventions or established norms. If you want permission from others before taking action, you will likely be waiting a long time or never receive it. But if you are willing to take risks and forge your own path, you can achieve great things.

To start getting things done with efficiency, try one of these tips.

181

1. DEFINE YOUR PURPOSE.

When Hopper started working with early electronic computers, she had a clear purpose: make software that would help people be more productive by automating as many repetitive tasks as possible when it came to programming computers. This guiding principle helped her stay motivated and focused, even when she encountered obstacles or setbacks.

In your own life and work, it is important to have a similar sense of purpose. What are you trying to achieve? Why does it matter to you? When you know the answers to these questions, it will be easier for you to take action and persevere when things get difficult.

Let's say you are a cashier, and you want to be more efficient in your job. One way to do this is by automating as many tasks as possible so that you can spend more time helping customers. So, you start by creating a list of all the tasks you currently do during your shift. Over the next several days, you look for ways to streamline or automate them. You consider a better way to organize your workspace, ways to speed up the checkout process, and how to handle customer questions more efficiently. Finally, you come up with a plan and implement it. After a few weeks, you have cut your average transaction time by thirty seconds, which saves the company money and makes your customers happy.

2. DO YOUR RESEARCH.

Hopper was a mathematician before joining the Naval Reserve and then working for early computer companies. As computers weren't publicly available or simply didn't exist yet, Hopper had to learn an entirely new field before putting into action her idea of coding computers in English. Indeed, she published several research papers in electrical engineering journals before creating the first compiler.

Before taking any action, it's important to do your homework and gather as much information as possible. This will help you understand the situation better and develop a plan of attack that has the best chance for success. Once you know what you want to do, take the time to learn as much as possible about the topic or issue at hand. This will give you a better understanding of the challenges involved and help you develop more creative solutions. It will also make it easier for you to convince others that your idea is worth pursuing.

Suppose you want to start a small business that combines your two passions: coffee and reading. You could rush to the bank and ask for a loan, but without doing any research first, you're likely to make some mistakes. So instead, you start by reading everything you can find about starting a coffee shop. You learn about the different types of business entities, how to choose a location, what type of equipment you need, and how to price your products. You also talk to people who have already started similar businesses and ask for advice. You decide on a unique pitch of a café that specializes in rare and vintage books, which you will initially sell on consignment, so you don't have to buy them outright. With a solid business plan in hand, you approach the bank and are approved for a loan.

3. TRY DIFFERENT APPROACHES UNTIL ONE WORKS.

Hopper wanted to program computers with English sentences rather than tedious machine code. However, she quickly realized that there is very little standardization in English, so it would be impossible. From there, she invented various high-level programming language specifications until she found one that could be both intuitive to human programmers and able to be compiled to the low-level code of the machine.

Sometimes the most direct approach isn't always the best—or easiest—way to get something done. If you find yourself hitting roadblocks, try thinking outside the box and approaching the problem from a different angle. Experimenting until you find an effective solution can be time-consuming, but it always pays off in the end.

Imagine you've made a resolution to improve your sleep. You start with the obvious plan of setting a bedtime routine, but after a few weeks, you find that you're still not falling asleep easily. So, you try a different approach and start taking melatonin an hour before bedtime. But after another week of restless nights, you realize that this isn't working, either. The easy solutions don't work, but you don't give up. You start doing some research on sleep and learn about the different stages of sleep cycles. You discover that it takes most people an average of fourteen minutes to fall asleep, so you start using a timer to track your progress. After a few nights of experimentation, you find that, if you relax for twenty minutes before getting into bed, drink chamomile tea, and read for ten minutes with dim lighting, you fall asleep in under fifteen minutes consistently.

THE SCIENCE

In large organizations, you may need to be the one to take action due to *diffusion of responsibility*. In a wide variety of contexts, researchers have shown that apathy can occur when one loses a sense of personal agency when responsibilities are distributed over a large group. In their classic work, Darley and Latané showed that people will take responsibility when no one else is around to act. Recognizing this, you may need to be the one to take action simply because human psychology dictates no one else will.

People also tend to actively avoid responsibility for fear of punishment. This blame avoidance results in the familiar phenomenon of "passing the buck." Research published in *Organizational Behavior and Human Decision Processes* found that people delegate choices for others more so than choices for themselves primarily to avoid responsibility rather than deferring to expertise. In other words, asking someone to give you permission is a form of potential blame-passing. By making the choice yourself, you have taken the responsibility and not forced that burden onto someone else.

It should go without saying that informed decision-making is important, but research continues to underscore this point. In medicine, the ultimate choice in treatment rests with the patient. But research shows that patient choices are heavily influenced by clinicians before seeing additional experts, pointing to the importance and power of information being obtained early on. While it might seem obvious that information is important, what counts as an informed evidence-based decision is anything but. Nutley, Powell, and Davies reviewed the evidence schemes of U.S. and UK governing bodies, and although there was no consensus on what counts as "good" information, it was clear that any criteria must be contextualized based on its use.

If you are making a simple decision, like what to eat for dinner, then "folk" knowledge about what tastes good is probably fine. However, if you are tasked with making a decision that will affect important stakeholders, then many forms of evidence, including expert knowledge, are warranted.

Hopper took the actions that she thought would help most people. You, too, can do this responsibly by first doing the research and then forging ahead with the best strategy.

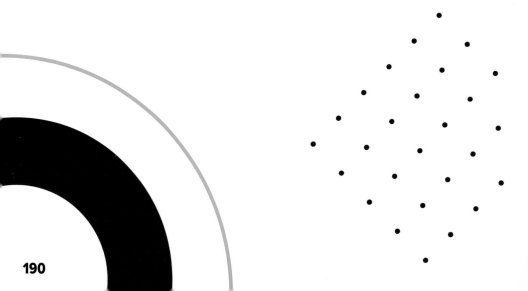

REFERENCES

Adolphs, Ralph. "The Biology of Fear." *Current Biology* CB23, no. 2 (2013): R79–R93. https://doi.org/10.1016/j.cub.2012.11.055.

Appe, Susan, and Allison Schnable. "Don't Reinvent the Wheel: Possibilities for and Limits to Building Capacity Of Grassroots International Ngos." *Third World Quarterly* 40, no. 10 (2019): 1832–1849. https://doi.org/10.1080/01436597.2019.1636226.

Baker, Wayne. *Achieving Success through Social Capital: Tapping the Hidden Resources in Your Personal and Business Networks.* San Francisco: Jossey-Bass, 2010. https://www.google.com/books/edition/Achieving_Success_Through_Social_Capital/ywEPAQAAMAAJ?hl=en.

Bandura, Albert. "Moral Disengagement in the Perpetration of Inhumanities." *Personality and Social Psychology Review* 3, no. 3 (1999): 193–209. https://doi.org/10.1207/s15327957pspr0303_3.

Berger, Warren. *A More Beautiful Question: The Power of Inquiry to Spark Breakthrough Ideas.* United States: Bloomsbury USA, 2014. https://www.google.com/books/edition/A_More_Beautiful_Question/CyLBAgAAQBAJ.

Bickford, Deborah J., and David Wright. *Community: The Hidden Context for Learning.* In *Learning Spaces*, edited by Diana G. Oblinger. University of

Dayton, 2006. https://www.educause.edu/research-and-publications/books/learning-spaces/chapter-4-community-hidden-context-learning.

Cabinet Office. "FY 2007 White Paper on the National Lifestyle: A Comfortable Way of Life for the Japanese People, Founded on Personal Relationships." 2007. http://www5.cao.go.jp/seikatsu/whitepaper/h19/10_pdf/01_honpen/.

Carleton, R. Nicolas, "Fear of the Unknown: One Fear to Rule Them All?" *Journal of Anxiety Disorders* 41(2016): 5–21. https://doi.org/10.1016/j.janxdis.2016.03.011.

Carver, Charles, Michael F. Scheier, and Suzanne C. Segerstrom. "Optimism." *Clinical Psychology Review* 30, no. 7 (2010): 879–889. https://doi.org/10.1016/j.cpr.2010.01.006.

Chambless, Diane, and Thomas Ollendick. "Empirically Supported Psychological Interventions: Controversies and Evidence." *Annual Review of Psychology* 52, no. 1 (2001): 685–716. https://doi.org/10.1146/annurev.psych.52.1.685.

Coutinho, M. V., J. Thomas, A. S. Alsuwaidi, and J. J. Couchman. "Dunning-Kruger Effect: Intuitive Errors Predict Overconfidence on the Cognitive Reflection Test." *Frontiers in Psychology* (2021): 1040. https://doi.org/10.1016/j.cortex.2021.01.015.

Csikszentmihalyi, Mihaly. *Flow: The Psychology of Happiness.* United Kingdom: Penguin Random House, 2022. https://www.google.com/books/edition/_/E51kzgEACAAJ.

Darley, J., and B. Latané. "Bystander Intervention in Emergencies: Diffusion of Responsibility." *Journal of Personality and Social Psychology* 8, no. 4p1 (1968): 377. https://psycnet.apa.org/doi/10.1037/h0025589.

Davis, Don E., Everett Worthington Jr., and Joshua Hook. "Humility: Review of Measurement Strategies and Conceptualization as a Personality Judgment." *Journal of Positive Psychology* 5 (2010): 243–252, https://doi.org/10.1080/17439761003791672.

Davidson, Janet E. "Insights about Insightful Problem Solving." In *Psychology of Problem Solving*, edited by Janet H. Davidson and Robert Sternberg. Cambridge: Cambridge University Press, 2003: 149–157. https://doi.org/10.1017/CBO9780511615771.006.

de Janasz, Suzanne, and Monica Forret. "Learning the Art of Networking: A Critical Skill for Enhancing Social Capital and Career Success." *Journal of Management Education* 32, no. 5 (2008): 629–650. https://doi.org/10.1177/1052562907307637.

Driessen, Erik, Karlijn Overeem, and Cees van der Vleuten. "Get Yourself a Mentor." *Medical Education* 45 (2011): 438–439. https://doi.org/10.1111/j.1365–2923.2011.03948.x.

Duckworth, Angela L., Teri A. Kirby, Eli Tsukayama, Heather Berstein, and Krampe Ericsson. "Deliberate Practice Spells Success: Why Grittier Competitors Triumph at the National Spelling Bee." *Social Psychological and Personality Science* 2, no. 2 (2011): 174–181. https://doi.org/10.1177/1948550610385872.

Dweck, Carol S. *Mindset: Changing the Way You Think to Fulfill Your Potential*, Revised edition. London: Robinson, 2017. https://www.google.com/books /edition/Mindset_Updated_Edition/ckoKDQAAQBAJ?hl=en.

Ebrahimi, Omid, Stale Pallesen, Robin Kenter, and Tine Nordgreen. "Psychological Interventions for the Fear of Public Speaking: A Meta-analysis." *Frontiers in Psychology* 10 (2019): 488. https://doi.org/10.3389/fpsyg.2019.00488.

Eller, Ryan. "Ikigai and Higher Education: A Review of the Literature." *AU EJournal of Interdisciplinary Research*, 2016. http://www.assumptionjournal .au.edu/index.php/eJIR/article/view/4278.

Epstein, Robert, Steven M. Schmidt, and Regina Warfel. "Measuring and Training Creativity Competencies: Validation of a New Test." *Creativity Research Journal* 20, no. 1 (2008): 7–12. https://doi.org/10.1080/10400410701839876.

Ericsson, K. Anders, and W. Kintsch. "Long-Term Working Memory." *Psychological Review* 102, no. 2 (1995): 211–245. https://doi.org/10.10 37/0033-295X.102.2.211.

Ericsson, K. Anders, Ralf T. Krampe, and Clemens Tesch-Römer. "The Role of Deliberate Practice in the Acquisition of Expert Performance." *Psychological Review* 100, no. 3 (1993): 63–406. https://psycnet.apa.org /record/1993-40718-001.

Ferriss, Timothy. *Tools of Titans: The Tactics, Routines, and Habits of Billionaires, Icons, and World-Class Performers*. United Kingdom: Ebury Publishing, 2016. https://www.google.com/books/edition/Tools_of_Titans/fjr3DAAAQBAJ.

Fischer, Melissa A., Kathleen Mazor, Joann Baril, Eric Alper, Deborah DeMarco, and Michele Puginaire. "Learning from Mistakes," *Journal of General Internal Medicine* 21 (2006): 419–423. https://doi.org/10.1111/j.1525-1497.2006.00420.x

German, Tim P., and Margaret A. Defeyter. "Immunity to Functional Fixedness in Young Children." *Psychonomic Bulletin & Review* 7 (2000): 707–712. https://doi.org/10.3758/BF03213010.

Gilhooly, Kenneth J. "Incubation and Intuition in Creative Problem Solving." *Frontiers in Psychology* 7 (2016): 1076. https://doi.org/10.3389/fpsyg.2016.01076.

Goodwill, Alicia, and Annabel Chen. "The Science of Lifelong Learning." *UNESCO Report* (2021). UIL/2021/PI/H/3. https://unesdoc.unesco.org/ark:/48223/pf0000377812.

Greenspon, Thomas S. "'Healthy Perfectionism' Is an Oxymoron!: Reflections on the Psychology of Perfectionism and the Sociology of Science." *Journal of Secondary Gifted Education* 11, no. 4 (2000): 197–208. https://www.researchgate.net/publication/284063973_Healthy_perfectionism_is_an_oxymoron_Reflections_on_the_psychology_of_perfectionism_and_the_sociology_of_science.

Grima, Francois, Pascal Paillé, Jorge Mejia, and Lionel Prud'homme. "Exploring the Benefits of Mentoring Activities for the Mentor." *Career Development International* 19, no. 4 (2014): 469–490. https://doi.org/10.1108/CDI-05-2012-0056.

Gruber, Matthias J., Bernard Gelman, and Charan Ranganath. "States of Curiosity Modulate Hippocampus-Dependent Learning Via the Dopaminergic Circuit." *Neuron* 84, no. 2 (2014): 486–496. https://doi.org/10.1016/j .neuron.2014.08.060.

Hammond, Cathie. "Impacts of Lifelong Learning upon Emotional Resilience, Psychological and Mental Health: Fieldwork Evidence." *Oxford Review of Education* 30, no. 4 (2004): 551–568. https://doi.org/10.1080/0305498042 000303008.

Hawkins, R. X., A. Stuhlmüller, Degen, J., and N. D. Goodman. "Why Do You Ask? Good Questions Provoke Informative Answers." *Cognitive Science* (2015). https://cogsci.mindmodeling.org/2015/papers/0158/.

Hsieh, Peggy, Jeremy Sullivan, and Norma Guerra. "A Closer Look at College Students: Self-efficacy and Goal Orientation." *Journal of Advanced Academics* 18, no. 3 (2007): 454–476. https://doi.org/10.4219/jaa-2007-500.

Ilgen, Jonathan, Keven Eva, Anique de Bruin, David A. Cook, and Glen Regehr. "Comfort with Uncertainty: Reframing Our Conceptions of How Clinicians Navigate Complex Clinical Situations." *Advances in Health Sciences Education* 24 (2019): 797–809. https://doi.org/10.1007/s10459-018-9859-5.

Jackson, Susan. A., and Herbert Marsh. "Development and Validation of a Scale to Measure Optimal Experience: The Flow State Scale." *Journal of Sport and Exercise Psychology* 18, no. 1 (1996): 17–35. https://doi.org/10.1123 /jsep.18.1.17.

Jia, Xin, Wenjie Zhou, Xu Sun, and Yunfang Wu. "How to Ask Good Questions? Try to Leverage Paraphrases." *Proceedings of the 58th Annual Meeting of the Association for Computational Linguistics* (2020): 6130–6140. https://doi.org/10.18653/v1/2020.acl-main.545.

Kircanski, Katherine, Matthew Lieberman, and Michelle Craske. "Feelings into Words: Contributions of Language to Exposure Therapy." *Psychological Science* 23, no. 10. (2012): 1086–1091. https://journals.sagepub.com/doi/10.1177/0956797612443830.

Kumano, Michiko. "On the Concept of Well-Being in Japan: Feeling Shiawase as Hedonic Well-Being and Feeling Ikigai as Eudaimonic Well-Being." *Applied Research Quality Life* 13 (2018): 419–433. https://doi.org/10.1007/s11482-017-9532-9.

Kushlev, Kostadin, and Elizabeth Dunn. "Checking Email Less Frequently Reduces Stress." *Computers in Human Behavior* 43: 220–228. https://doi.org/10.1016/j.chb.2014.11.005.

Kushlev, Kostadin, Jason Proulx, and Elizabeth Dunn. "Silence Your Phones': Smartphone Notifications Increase Inattention and Hyperactivity Symptoms." *Proceedings of the 2016 CHI Conference on Human Factors in Computing Systems*: 1011–1020. https://doi.org/10.1145/2858036.2858359.

Langa, Kenneth, Eric Larson, Eileen Crimmins, Jessica Faul, Deborah Levine, Mohammed Kabeto, and David Weir. "A Comparison of the Prevalence of Dementia in the United States in 2000 and 2012." *JAMA Internal Medicine* 177, no. 1 (2017): 51–58. https://doi.org/10.1001/jamainternmed.2016.6807.

Liu, Lu, Yang Wang, Roberta Sinatra, C. Lee Giles, Chaoming Song, and Dashun Wang. "Hot Streaks in Artistic, Cultural, and Scientific Careers." *Nature* 559, no. 7714 (2018): 396–399. https://doi.org/10.1038/s41586-018-0315-8.

Macnamara, Brooke, David Z. Hambrick, and Frederick Oswald. "Deliberate Practice and Performance in Music, Games, Sports, Education, and Professions: A Meta-Analysis." *Psychological Science* 25, no. 8 (2014): 1608–1618. https://journals.sagepub.com/doi/10.1177/0956797614535810.

Mahoney, Alison, and Peter McEvoy. "Changes in Intolerance of Uncertainty During Cognitive Behavior Group Therapy for Social Phobia." *Journal of Behavior Therapy and Experimental Psychiatry* 43, no. 2 (2012): 849–854, https://doi.org/10.1016/j.jbtep.2011.12.004.

Manohar, Sanjay, Patricia Lockwood, Daniel Drew, Sean Fallon, Trevor Chong, Sanjeeva Jeyaretna, Ian Baker, et al. "Reduced Decision Bias and More Rational Decision Making Following Ventromedial Prefrontal Cortex Damage." *Cortex* 138 (2021): 24–37. https://doi.org/10.1016/j.cortex.2021.01.015.

Masia, Bertram, Benjamin Bloom, and David R. Krathwohl. *Taxonomy of Educational Objectives: The Classification of Educational Goals.* United Kingdom: Longmans, Green, 1956. https://www.google.com/books/edition/Taxonomy_of_Educational_Objectives/rJNqAAAAMAAJ.

Newman, MEJ. "Power Laws, Pareto Distributions and Zipf's Law." *Contemporary Physics* 46, no. 5 (2005): 323–351. https://doi.org/10.1080/00107510500052444.

Nutley, S., A. Powell, and H. Davies. "What Counts as Good Evidence?" *Provocation Paper for the Alliance for Useful Evidence*. London: Alliance for Useful Evidence, 2013. http://hdl.handle.net/10023/3518.

O'Keefe, Paul, Carol Dweck, and Gregory Walton. "Implicit Theories of Interest: Finding Your Passion or Developing It?" *Psychological Science* 29, no. 10 (2018): 1653–1664. https://doi.org/10.1177/0956797618780643.

Pascual-Leone, Alvaro, Amir Amedi, Felipe Fregni, and Lotfi Merabet. "The Plastic Human Brain Cortex." *Annual Review of Neuroscience* 28, no. 1 (2005): 377–401. https://doi.org/10.1146/annurev.neuro.27.070203.144216.

Proyer, Rene, Willibald Ruch, Numan Ali, Hmoud Olimat, Toshihiko Amemiya, Tamirie Adal, Sadia Ansari, et al. "Breaking Ground in Cross-Cultural Research on the Fear of Being Laughed at (Gelotophobia): A Multinational Study Involving 73 Countries." *Humor: International Journal of Humor Research* 22, no. 1–2 (2009): 253–279. https://doi.org/10.1515/HUMR.2009.012.

Radicati, S., and J. Levenstein. "Email Statistics Report, 2015–2019." Radicati Group, Palo Alto, CA, USA, Tech. Rep. https://www.radicati.com/wp /wp-content/uploads/2015/02/Email-Statistics-Report-2015–2019 -Executive-Summary.pdf.

Rincones, Orlando, Mark Sidhom, Pascal Mancuso, Karen Wong, Megan Berry, Dion Forstner, Leslie Bokey, et al. "Robot or Radiation? A Qualitative Study of the Decision Support Needs of Men with Localised Prostate Cancer Choosing Between Robotic Prostatectomy and Radiotherapy Treatment."

Patient Education and Counseling 102, no. 7 (2019): 1364–1372. https://doi
.org/10.1016/j.pec.2019.02.017.

Rohrer, Julia, Warren Tierney, Eric Uhlmann, Lisa DeBruine, Tom Heyman, Benedict Jones, Stefan Schmukle, et al. "Putting the Self in Self-Correction: Findings from the Loss-of-Confidence Project." *Perspectives on Psychological Science* 16, no. 6: 1255–1269. https://doi.org/10.1177/1745691620964106.

Roth, Wolff-Micahel, and Michiel Van Eijck, "Fullness of Life as Minimal Unit: Science, Technology, Engineering, and Mathematics (STEM) Learning across the Life Span." *Science Education* 94 (2010): 1027–1048. https://doi
.org/10.1002/sce.20401.

Rothe, A., B. M. Lake, and T. M. Gureckis. "Do People Ask Good Questions?." *Computational Brain & Behavior* 1 (2018): 69–89. https://doi.org/10.1007
/s42113-018-0005-5.

Schnitker, Sarah, and Robert Emmons. "Patience as a Virtue: Religious and Psychological Perspectives." *Research in the Social Scientific Study of Religion* 18 (2007). https://doi.org/10.1163/ej.9789004158511.i-301.69.

Seligman, Martine, Peter Schulman, and Alyssa M. Tryon. "Group Prevention of Depression and Anxiety Symptoms." *Behavior Research and Therapy* 45 (2007): 1111–1126. https://doi.org/10.1016/j.brat.2006.09.010.

Soon, Chun, Marcel Brass, Hans-Jochen Heinze and John-Dylan Haynes. "Unconscious Determinants of Free Decisions in the Human Brain." *Nature Neuroscience* 11 (2008): 543–545. https://doi.org/10.1038/nn.2112.

Steffel, Mary, Elanor F. Williams, and Jaclyn Perrmann-Graham. "Passing the Buck: Delegating Choices to Others to Avoid Responsibility and Blame." *Organizational Behavior and Human Decision Processes* 135 (2016): 32. https://doi.org/10.1016/j.obhdp.2016.04.006.

Stephens, A. L., and John Clement. "The Role of Thought Experiments in Science and Science Learning." *Second International Handbook of Science Education. Springer International Handbooks of Education* 24 (2012). https://doi.org/10.1007/978-1-4020-9041-7_13.

van der Klink, Marcel, and Jan Streumer, "Effectiveness of On-the-Job Training," *Journal of European Industrial Training* 26, no. 2/3/4 (2002): 196–199. https://doi.org/10.1108/03090590210422076.

West, Richard, and Gregory Williams. "'I Don't Think That Word Means What You Think It Means': A Proposed Framework for Defining Learning Communities." *Educational Technology Research and Development* vol. 65 (2017): 1569–1582. https://doi.org/10.1007/s11423-017-9535-0.

Wills, A. J., A. Lavric, G. S. Croft, and T. L. Hodgson. "Predictive Learning, Prediction Errors, and Attention: Evidence from Event-Related Potentials and Eye Tracking." *Journal of Cognitive Neuroscience* 19, no. 5 (2007): 843–854. https://doi.org/10.1162/jocn.2007.19.5.843.

Wiseman, Richard. *The Luck Factor*. United Kingdom: Arrow, 2004. https://www.google.com/books/edition/The_Luck_Factor/WmmUYCvxhNEC?hl=en.

Woods, Majka, and Mark Rosenberg. "Educational Tools: Thinking Outside the Box," *CJASN* vol. 11 (2016): 518. https://cjasn.asnjournals.org/content/11/3/518.

Yablonski, Jon. *Laws of UX: Using Psychology to Design Better Products & Services.* Sebastopol, CA O'Reilly Media, 2020. https://www.google.com/books/edition/Laws_of_UX/BuneDwAAQBAJ.

Yeager, David, Paul Hanselman, Gregory M. Walton, Jared S., Murray, Robert Crosnoe, Chandra Muller, Elizabeth Tipton, et al. "A National Experiment Reveals Where a Growth Mindset Improves Achievement." *Nature* 573 (2019): 364–369. https://doi.org/10.1038/s41586-019-1466-y.

Zou, Xi, and Paul Ingram. "Bonds and Boundaries: Network Structure, Organizational Boundaries, and Job Performance." *Organizational Behavior and Human Decision Processes* 120, no. 1 (2013): 98–109. https://doi.org/10.1016/j.obhdp.2012.09.002.

ACKNOWLEDGMENTS

I thank my family for giving me the inspiration to write. I am grateful to Lindsay for tirelessly proofreading and providing many suggestions for improving this book. Thanks goes to my editor, Meg Gibbons, and her team for their patience and skill in helping me shape and refine this book. I am also deeply indebted to all the scientists and researchers who have dedicated their lives to understanding the natural world, giving us excellent role models to follow.

ABOUT THE AUTHOR

Chris Ferrie obtained his PhD in mathematics at the University of Waterloo in 2012 and now lives in Brisbane, Australia, with his wife and four children. During the day, he is an associate professor at the University of Technology Sydney, where he researches and lectures on quantum physics, computation, and engineering. Ferrie is the author of *Quantum Bullsh*t: How to Ruin Your Life with Quantum Physics*, and with titles such as *Quantum Physics for Babies*, he is also the number one bestselling science author for kids.